I0817514

NORTH AMERICAN FIELD GUIDES

# MAMMALS

Carla Mooney

Field Guides

An Imprint of Abdo Reference | abdobooks.com

# CONTENTS

## Hares, Pikas, and Rabbits



## Rodents



## Moles and Shrews



## Armadillos and Opossums



## Sea Mammals

# WHAT ARE MAMMALS?

Mammals are some of the most diverse animals on Earth. They can be as tiny as a mouse or as massive as a blue whale. More than 6,000 species of mammals live on Earth. Every continent and ocean has mammals living there. Mammals live in jungles, deserts, grasslands, tundra, woodlands, mountains, fresh water, and oceans.

Mammals move in many ways. They walk, run, climb, jump, scurry, swing, dig, swim, dive, and fly. Some mammals are meat-eating carnivores, while others are plant-eating herbivores. Mammals that are omnivores eat both meat and plants.

Some mammals, such as porcupines and polar bears, spend most of their lives alone. Others, such as wolves and dolphins, live in family groups. Still others, such as deer and wild horses, live in large social groups. There are benefits to living in social groups. The group can share the responsibility of raising offspring. Large groups provide protection from predators and more opportunities to find a mate. For predators, hunting with a group can help bring down large prey.

## CHARACTERISTICS OF MAMMALS

All mammals are vertebrates, which means they have a backbone. They breathe air. Their bodies can keep a steady temperature even as their environments warm up or cool down. And most mammals give birth to live young.

Mammals have four characteristics that separate them from other animal groups. First, mammals feed their young milk, which is produced in mammary glands. The milk provides nutrients that help the young grow and develop.

Second, all mammals have hair or fur at some point. Mammal hair can be long, short, coarse, soft, thick, or thin. Hair protects mammals' skin from the sun. It keeps mammals warm in cold temperatures. A polar bear needs its thick fur coat to stay warm. Sometimes a mammal's hair helps it blend into its environment. Some hairs, such as a cat's whiskers, help mammals sense the world around them.

Third, mammals have a unique jaw. Their hinged jaw attaches directly to their skull. Finally, mammals have three small bones in the middle ear. These bones transmit sound for hearing.

Mammals come in many shapes, sizes, and colors. They have adapted to live in hot, cold, wet, and dry environments. With such diversity, mammals are some of the most fascinating animals on Earth.

# HOW TO USE THIS BOOK

**Tab shows the mammal category.**

**The mammal's common name appears here.**

RODENTS

## GROUNDHOG *(MARMOTA MONAX)*

The groundhog is also called a woodchuck. This common rodent has a heavy body with short, powerful legs and a short, fluffy tail. The groundhog's fur is brownish and grizzled. When startled, groundhogs make a shrill whistle call. Groundhogs dig burrows in slopes or banks near the edges of woodlands. A burrow usually has multiple entrances. During the day, groundhogs hunt for food or relax in the sun near the burrow entrance. Although they eat pr[i]marily native grasses and flowering plants, groundhogs th[a]t live near humans sometimes raid vegetable gardens. [I]n winter, groundhogs hibernate in their burrows.

**This paragraph gives information about the mammal.**

### HOW TO SPOT

**Size:** 20 to 34 inches (51 to 86 cm) long including tail; 4 to 14 pounds (1.8 to 6.4 kg)

**...American Range:** ...Canada, and ...and central ...States

**...:** Fields, ...vs, woodland ...gs, and urban and suburban yards

**Diet:** Grasses, flowering plants, clover, alfalfa, garden crops, and other plants

### GROUNDHOG DAY

German immigrants brought the tradition of using rodents to predict the weather to the United States. In 1877 the first Groundhog Day celebration was held in Punxsutawney, Pennsylvania. According to legend, if the groundhog comes out of its burrow on February 2 and sees its shadow, there will be six more weeks of winter. Spring will come early if the ... does not see its shadow.

76

**Sidebars provide additional information about the topic.**

## OUSE MOUSE *(MUS MUSCULUS)*

e house mouse is a small rodent with a pointed nose
ge, rounded ears. Its long tail is nearly hairless. Its fu
nges from light brown to black with a lighter underbe
ouse mice have strong hearing, sight, and smell. Thei
hiskers help them feel surfaces and air movement. Th
ice often live in underground burrows or in cracks in
ocks or walls. They build nests from soft materials suc
paper and rags. Most house mice are nocturnal but can be
active during the day. They run fast and are skilled climbers
and jumpers.

**The mammal's scientific name appears here.**

### HOW TO SPOT

**Size:** 4.9 to 7.9 inches (12.5 to 20 cm) long including tail; 0.4 to 1 ounce (11 to 28 g)

**North American Range:** Across North America

**Habitat:** Places ne humans, such as houses, barns, fie and other building

**Diet:** Leaves, root seeds, grains, nu fruits, insects, ca and arthropods

***How to Spot*** **boxes give information about the mammal's size, range, habitat, and diet. Height is always measured to the shoulders.**

### FUN FACT

**Male mice can sing and change the notes in their song. However, their song is too high a frequency for humans to hear.**

**Images show the mammal.**

***Fun Facts*** **give interesting information about mammals.**

# AMERICAN BISON *(BISON BISON)*

The American bison is North America's largest land animal. It has a massive head and a large hump on its shoulders. Its deep brown fur grows long around its head and face. Adult bison have short, black horns that curve up from their head. Males use their horns or bump heads to fight. American bison live in herds. They communicate by smell and sound. Their sounds include grunting, snorting, and growling. Bison spend most of their time grazing on plants and grasses. In the winter, they use their large heads to clear away snow to find food.

## HOW TO SPOT

**Size:** 5 to 6.5 feet (1.5 to 2 m) tall; 1,800 to 2,400 pounds (820 to 1,090 kg)

**North American Range:** Canada, Alaska, and northwestern United States

**Habitat:** Open plains, grasslands, and savannas

**Diet:** Low-growing grasses and sedges

## BIGHORN SHEEP *(OVIS CANADENSIS)*

The bighorn sheep is muscular. It is brown with white around its mouth, belly, and rear. As its name suggests, the male bighorn sheep has a pair of large, curved horns that can weigh up to 30 pounds (14 kg). Females have smaller horns. Bighorn sheep hit cacti with their horns, breaking open the cacti so the sheep can eat the flesh inside. The sheep also fight with their horns. Their hooves help them grip and climb the steep mountain terrain where they live. Bighorn sheep have great sight, smell, and hearing, which help them sense and escape predators such as coyotes, golden eagles, cougars, and bears.

### HOW TO SPOT

**Size:** 2.5 to 3.25 feet (0.8 to 1 m) tall; 100 to 220 pounds (45 to 100 kg)

**North American Range:** Western North America

**Habitat:** Mountain ranges

**Diet:** Plants such as grasses, sedges, and clover

Male

Female

### FUN FACT

Bighorn sheep in groups stand facing different directions so they can watch for approaching predators.

# CARIBOU *(RANGIFER TARANDUS)*

Caribou are members of the deer family. They live in northern regions of North America. Caribou have brown hair with white patches on the neck, rump, and feet. They are the only deer species in which both males and females grow antlers. Every year, the antlers fall off. They grow back bigger. Caribou use their large hooves to paddle through water and dig in the snow for food. The hooves also help caribou grip and stand on rocks or ice. Caribou live in herds that constantly move to find food. In summer, the herds migrate north to grazing grounds. When the first snow falls, the herd migrates south to its winter grazing grounds. Some herds travel more than 600 miles (966 km).

## HOW TO SPOT

**Size:** 3.6 to 4.6 feet (1.1 to 1.4 m) tall; 240 to 500 pounds (109 to 227 kg)

**North American Range:** Alaska and other northern regions of North America

**Habitat:** Arctic tundra, mountain tundra, and northern forests

**Diet:** Sedges, lichens, mosses, small shrubs, and other plants

# DALL SHEEP *(OVIS DALLI)*

Dall sheep are easily recognized by their white fur and the male sheep's enormous curled horns. Males, called rams, grow their distinctive horns around age three. The horns grow most of the year. In late fall and winter, growth slows and stops. The cycle of horn growth begins again in the spring. Females, called ewes, have shorter horns that are slightly curved. Dall sheep feed and rest on mountain ridges, in meadows, and on slopes. They move to rocks and crags to escape predators such as wolves, brown bears, and coyotes.

Female

Male

## HOW TO SPOT

**Size:** 3 to 3.5 feet (0.9 to 1.1 m) tall; 101 to 249 pounds (46 to 113 kg)

**North American Range:** Alaska and northern Canada

**Habitat:** Mountains

**Diet:** Sedges, lichens, mosses, grasses, and other plants

**FUN FACT**

The pattern of rings on a Dall sheep's horns can help determine the animal's age.

# DONKEY *(EQUUS ASINUS)*

Donkeys are hardy animals known for their strength and endurance. Donkeys are usually smaller than horses. They have long ears and a short, upright mane. These hoofed mammals make a distinctive braying call. They can navigate difficult terrain. Donkeys are not native to North America. Europeans brought domestic donkeys to the Americas starting in the 1400s. Some escaped or were set loose. They have become invasive in some areas. Donkeys often live in herds. One wild male typically leads a herd of several females. Donkeys usually move around to graze in the mornings and evenings. They rest at midday when temperatures are hottest.

## FUN FACT

**The donkey is sometimes called a burro, which is the Spanish word for donkey.**

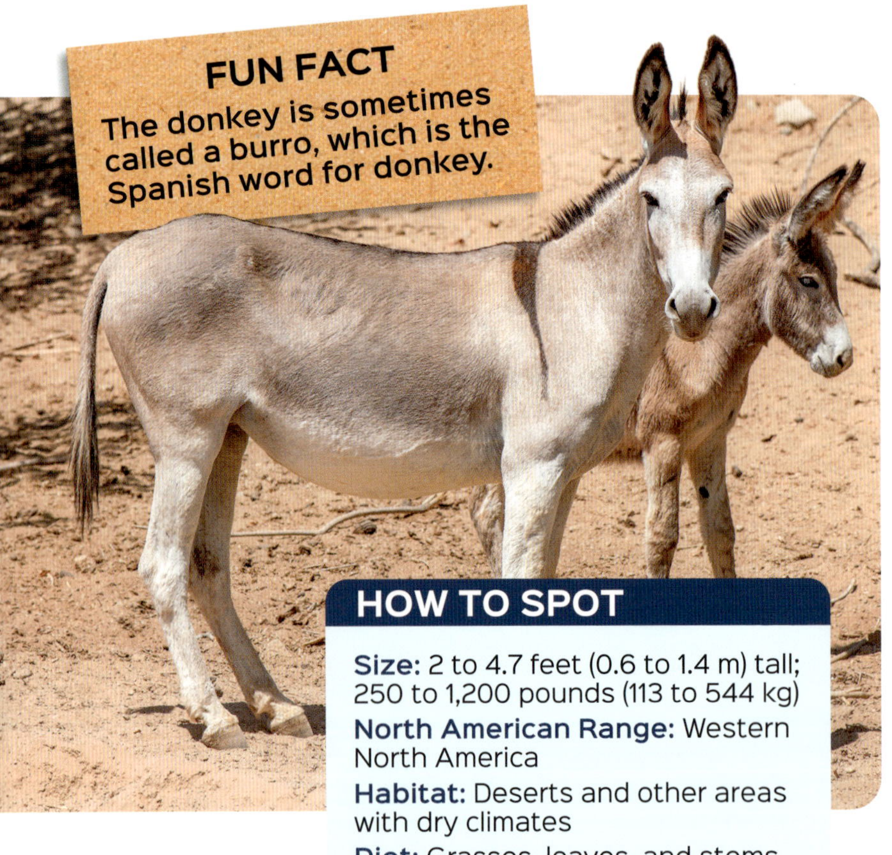

## HOW TO SPOT

**Size:** 2 to 4.7 feet (0.6 to 1.4 m) tall; 250 to 1,200 pounds (113 to 544 kg)

**North American Range:** Western North America

**Habitat:** Deserts and other areas with dry climates

**Diet:** Grasses, leaves, and stems

# ELK *(CERVUS CANADENSIS)*

Elk are the second-largest type of deer in the world. They have long legs and a short tail. In the winter, elk are light brown. They grow a long, dark-brown mane from the neck to the chest. In the summer, elk darken to a reddish tan. The mane gets thinner. Male elk have large antlers that shed and regrow each year. Elk are social animals and live in herds, which provide protection from predators such as wolves and bears.

## HOW TO SPOT

**Size:** 4.5 to 5 feet (1.4 to 1.5 m) tall; 400 to 800 pounds (181 to 363 kg)

**North American Range:** Western North America

**Habitat:** Grasslands, meadows, and forests

**Diet:** Grasses, sedges, leaves, branches, and other plants

Male

Female with winter mane

**FUN FACT**

An elk's new antlers are covered in a fuzzy skin called velvet, which holds nerves and blood vessels.

# HORSE *(EQUUS CABALLUS)*

The horse has a muscular torso supported by long, thin legs. A mane of coarse hair grows from the top of its large, elongated head down the back of its thick neck. The horse also has a long tail of hair. The horse's coat varies in color and pattern. Horses are not native to North America. Domestic horses came with Europeans starting in the 1400s. Some were set loose or escaped. They became wild. A male leads a herd of wild horses. The herd includes females, called mares, and young foals. Male foals are called colts. Around age two, colts leave the group and travel with other colts until they find their own groups of mares.

## HOW TO SPOT

**Size:** 2.5 to 5.8 feet (0.8 to 1.8 m) tall; 120 to 2,200 pounds (54 to 998 kg)

**North American Range:** Parts of Canada, United States, and Mexico

**Habitat:** Grasslands, steppes, savannas, and woodlands

**Diet:** Grasses, leaves, grains, wood, bark, and stems

# MOOSE *(ALCES ALCES)*

The moose is the biggest species of deer. It lives in forests across colder regions of North America. The moose's hair color ranges from dark brown to reddish or grayish brown. Each hair is hollow and filled with air. This air insulates the animal. The moose has a dewlap, or a flap of loose skin on its throat. Males have large, branched antlers that can grow up to six feet (1.8 m) across. The antlers drop in the fall and regrow in the spring. Male moose use their antlers to defend against predators.

Male

## HOW TO SPOT

**Size:** 5 to 7 feet (1.5 to 2.1 m) tall; 700 to 1,400 pounds (318 to 635 kg)

**North American Range:** Alaska, Canada, northern United States, Utah, and Colorado

**Habitat:** Forested areas in cold climates

**Diet:** Plants, twigs, leaves, bark, and shrubs

**FUN FACT**

**Female moose protect their young with fierce kicks that can break bones or kill predators.**

Female

# MOUNTAIN GOAT

## *(OREAMNOS AMERICANUS)*

Mountain goats live in the mountains of western North America. They have white coats. Mountain goats do not shed their shiny black horns. Each winter, a new growth ring is added to the horns. These growth rings can be used to estimate a goat's age. Mountain goats have a long, shaggy winter coat that keeps them warm. The goats shed their thick winter fur for short, sleek summer coats. Mountain goats are good climbers. Their hooves have a hard sheath and a soft pad. Both help the goat grip and climb on steep, rocky, and slippery ground.

### HOW TO SPOT

**Size:** 3.3 feet (1 m) tall; 130 to 260 pounds (59 to 118 kg) or more

**North American Range:** South-central Alaska to the Rocky Mountains in US northwest

**Habitat:** Mountains

**Diet:** Sedges, low shrubs, blueberries, hemlocks, forbs, and lichens

# MULE DEER *(ODOCOILEUS HEMIONUS)*

The mule deer has large ears and a distinct black forehead on a light-gray face. The deer goes from brownish tan in the summer to brownish gray in the winter. It has white fur on its rump. Its short tail is mostly white with a black tip. When running, mule deer leap with all four hooves off the ground at once. This motion is called stotting. Mule deer are herbivores but are selective in the plants they eat. They eat mainly plants dense in nutrients instead of lower-quality grasses.

Female, winter coat

Male, summer coat

## HOW TO SPOT

**Size:** 3 to 3.5 feet (0.9 to 1.1 m) tall; 130 to 280 pounds (59 to 127 kg)

**North American Range:** West of the Missouri River, especially the Rocky Mountains

**Habitat:** Dry, rocky environments

**Diet:** Herbaceous plants and the leaves and twigs of woody shrubs

# MUSK OX *(OVIBOS MOSCHATUS)*

The musk ox lives in the frozen Arctic. It has a long, shaggy, dark-brown coat with lighter hair on the forehead, legs, and saddle areas. The animal's hair keeps it warm in the cold climate. The coat's outer hairs, called guard hairs, can hang almost to the ground. The outer hairs grow over a shorter undercoat that insulates the musk ox in winter. After winter, the musk ox sheds its undercoat. A male musk ox's horns grow larger than a female's horns. A herd consists of about 24 to 36 musk oxen. When threatened, the herd forms a circle with the young in the middle and horns facing out toward predators.

## HOW TO SPOT

**Size:** 4 to 5 feet (1.2 to 1.5 m) tall; 550 to 750 pounds (250 to 340 kg)

**North American Range:** Northeastern Alaska and some parts of western Alaska

**Habitat:** Arctic tundra

**Diet:** Grasses, sedges, forbs, and woody plants

# PECCARY *(FAMILY TAYASSUIDAE)*

A peccary is a pig-like animal with a large head and round nose. Its coarse hair is dark brown or gray. The peccary has small tusks that grow straight. It has small ears and a small tail that is hard to see. Three species of peccaries live in North America. The most common is the collared peccary, which lives in the United States. The peccary's strong sense of smell and sturdy snout help it find and dig for food in the soil. Peccaries can swim and make large mudholes called wallows.

## HOW TO SPOT

**Size:** 1 to 4.6 feet (0.3 to 1.4 m) tall; 33 to 93 pounds (15 to 42 kg)

**North American Range:** Southwestern United States to Panama

**Habitat:** Rainforests, grasslands, deserts, woodlands, swamps, and mangroves

**Diet:** Fruits, seeds, roots, grasses, leaves, fungi, worms, grubs, small vertebrates, and eggs

## SEED DISPERSAL

Peccaries have an important role in a habitat. As the animals move around to new areas, they spit out seeds, release seeds in their waste, and drop seeds attached to their fur. Some of these seeds sprout and grow into new plants.

# PRONGHORN *(ANTILOCAPRA AMERICANA)*

Pronghorn look similar to deer. They have a long head and long legs. Their fur is reddish brown to dark brown with white markings on the neck, face, stomach, and rump. Their short horns grow straight up and curve backward. This animal is named for the fronts of its horns, which each have a small prong, or hook. The pronghorn is North America's fastest land animal, running nearly 60 miles per hour (97 kmh). Its excellent eyesight allows it to see predators from far away. When a pronghorn spots danger, it raises the white hairs on its rump as a signal to other pronghorn.

## HOW TO SPOT

**Size:** 3 to 5 feet (0.9 to 1.5 m) tall; 77 to 154 pounds (35 to 70 kg)

**North American Range:** Southern Canada to northern Mexico

**Habitat:** Plains, fields, grasslands, deserts, and basins

**Diet:** Grasses, forbs, sagebrush, and other plants

# WHITE-TAILED DEER

## *(ODOCOILEUS VIRGINIANUS)*

White-tailed deer are the smallest North American deer. Adults have a reddish-brown coat in summer that changes to grayish brown in winter. Males, called bucks, have large antlers that grow each year and shed in the winter. White-tailed deer typically are most active at dawn and dusk. These deer can sprint up to 30 miles per hour (48 kmh) and leap ten feet (3 m) high. They use their speed to escape predators such as bobcats, cougars, and coyotes.

**Male, *top*, and female, *bottom***

### HOW TO SPOT

**Size:** 6 to 8 feet (1.8 to 2.4 m) tall; 110 to 300 pounds (50 to 136 kg)

**North American Range:** Southern Canada to Central America

**Habitat:** Fields, meadows, and forests

**Diet:** Leaves, twigs, fruits, nuts, grasses, and other plants

# ARCTIC FOX *(VULPES LAGOPUS)*

The Arctic fox lives in the frigid Arctic region. Arctic foxes have thick fur that keeps them warm. Even their feet are covered in dense fur. When sleeping, the Arctic fox wraps its long, fluffy tail around its body like a blanket for warmth. In winter, its coat is white, blending into the snow and ice. This helps it avoid predators such as wolves, polar bears, and golden eagles. The fox's coat turns gray or brown in the summer, blending in with the tundra's rocks and plants. Arctic foxes dig and live in burrows or snow dens.

Winter coat

## HOW TO SPOT

**Size:** Average 1 foot (0.3 m) tall; 3 to 20 pounds (1.4 to 9.1 kg)

**North American Range:** Western Alaska through northern Canada

**Habitat:** Arctic and alpine tundra in coastal areas north of where trees stop growing

**Diet:** Small rodents, birds, fish, insects, and vegetables

Summer coat

# COYOTE *(CANIS LATRANS)*

The coyote is the size of a medium dog, with a slender body, bushy tail, and coarse hair that ranges from gray to reddish brown. Coyotes live in groups called packs. They are most active at dusk and dawn and are known for their distinctive howls at night. They howl to communicate with pack members and mark territory. As a pack, these intelligent canines work together and use their strong senses of smell and hearing to hunt prey. Packs also work together to raise young and protect their territory.

## HOW TO SPOT

**Size:** 1.5 to 2 feet (0.5 to 0.6 m) tall; 20 to 35 pounds (9.1 to 16 kg)

**North American Range:** Across North America

**Habitat:** Forests, grasslands, prairies, and deserts, from rural to urban areas

**Diet:** Deer, rabbits, rodents, frogs, fish, insects, and carrion

## CARRION FOR DINNER

Most carnivores hunt and kill the prey they eat. Some carnivores, including coyotes, eat dead or decaying animal material called carrion. Animals who eat this way are called scavengers. Many scavengers hunt mainly live prey. However, they also eat animals killed by another animal or that have died of natural causes, especially when food sources are scarce.

# EASTERN WOLF *(CANIS LYCAON)*

The eastern wolf roams the forests near the Great Lakes of southern Canada and the northern United States. Eastern wolves are in between the sizes of coyotes and gray wolves. They commonly have grayish-brown fur with a lighter cream color on the flanks and chest. Eastern wolves are social and live together in packs. A dominant male and female pair lead the pack, which includes their offspring. The wolves call to each other by howling, which can be heard miles away.

## HOW TO SPOT

**Size:** 2 to 3 feet (0.6 to 0.9 m) tall; 53 to 67 pounds (24 to 30 kg)

**North American Range:** Near the Great Lakes and Saint Lawrence River regions of northern United States and southern Canada

**Habitat:** Forests

**Diet:** White-tailed deer, moose, and beavers

# GRAY FOX *(UROCYON CINEREOARGENTEUS)*

The gray fox is a small forest predator with a narrow muzzle and large ears. It is recognized by its grizzled gray coat, reddish-brown legs, and black-tipped tail. The gray fox climbs trees to hunt or escape predators. To climb, the fox wraps its front legs around a tree trunk. It pushes up with its hind legs. Gray foxes are elusive and rarely seen in the daylight. They hide in dens, hollow trees or logs, thick brush, and sometimes underground burrows.

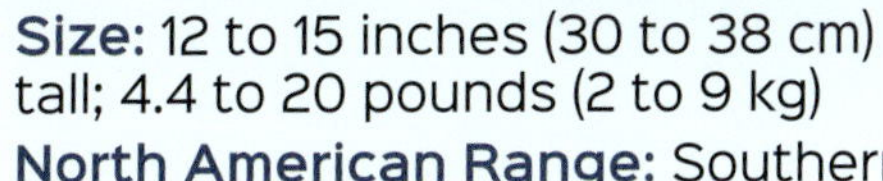

## HOW TO SPOT

**Size:** 12 to 15 inches (30 to 38 cm) tall; 4.4 to 20 pounds (2 to 9 kg)

**North American Range:** Southern Canada, United States, Mexico, and Central America

**Habitat:** Forests

**Diet:** Squirrels, birds, small rodents, rabbits, bird eggs, and fruits

# GRAY WOLF *(CANIS LUPUS)*

The gray wolf is the largest wild canine. Its coat is usually gray and brown but can include some white or black. Gray wolves have long legs that help them cover large areas quickly to find food. Their big, powerful jaws help them catch and eat large mammals. Like other wolves, gray wolves live in packs. They use their excellent sight, hearing, and smell to find prey and to find other members of the pack if they spread out.

## HOW TO SPOT

**Size:** 2 to 3 feet (0.6 to 0.9 m) tall; 60 to 145 pounds (27 to 66 kg)

**North American Range:** Alaska and parts of northwestern and north-central United States

**Habitat:** Tundra, woodlands, forests, grasslands, and deserts

**Diet:** Deer, elk, bison, moose, and other mammals

# KIT FOX *(VULPES MACROTIS)*

The kit fox is North America's smallest fox. These cat-sized foxes have adapted to live in desert environments. They have large ears that release heat to help the foxes stay cool. Their grayish-tan coats provide camouflage from predators and prey. The fur on their paws provides traction on the desert sand and protects the foxes from extreme heat. The nocturnal kit fox stays in its den during the day and comes out to hunt at night. Kit foxes are carnivorous, eating primarily small rodents and rabbits.

## HOW TO SPOT

**Size:** 9 to 12 inches (23 to 30 cm) tall; 4 to 5 pounds (1.8 to 2.3 kg)

**North American Range:** Southwestern United States to central Mexico

**Habitat:** Deserts and flat, dry lands with bushes and scrub

**Diet:** Small rodents, rabbits, carrion, and fruits

# RED FOX *(VULPES VULPES)*

Red foxes are solitary hunters known for their intelligence and cunning. Their fur is primarily red, with grayish-white fur on the throat, chin, and belly. The red fox has black feet. Its large, pointy ears are also tipped in black. The fox's fluffy, white-tipped tail is used for balance and warmth. The red fox has adapted to live near humans, making its home in parks and at the edges of woodlands. It eats whatever is available, sometimes stealing food from garbage cans and farms.

## HOW TO SPOT

**Size:** Average 15.7 inches (40 cm) tall; 6.5 to 24 pounds (2.9 to 11 kg)

**North American Range:** Northern Canada to Central America

**Habitat:** Woodlands, wetlands, fields, and rural and suburban neighborhoods

**Diet:** Rodents, rabbits, birds, amphibians, and fruits

## RED WOLF *(CANIS RUFUS)*

The red wolf has a reddish-gray coat. The fur is most red on the head, ears, and legs. These wolves are highly intelligent and social. They communicate through a variety of barks, growls, and howls. Their howls carry for several miles. The red wolf lives in a pack of two to ten wolves. Red wolves are very territorial, defending their territory from other animals. They are nocturnal and hunt mainly at night. The wolves hunt in packs. They travel up to 20 miles (32 km) per day looking for food.

### HOW TO SPOT

**Size:** 2.2 to 2.6 feet (0.7 to 0.8 m) tall; 45 to 80 pounds (20 to 36 kg)

**North American Range:** Southeastern United States

**Habitat:** Coastal prairies and marshes

**Diet:** Deer, raccoons, and small mammals

# BOBCAT *(LYNX RUFUS)*

The bobcat is a medium-sized cat that has light-gray to brown fur with a lighter underside. Bobcats have patterns of spots or stripes on their bodies. The patterns help bobcats blend into their environment when they hunt prey. The bobcat also has a facial ruff, which is a ring of fur surrounding its face. Its ears have tufts at the tips and two white spots on the back. The spots help kittens follow their mother in low light. The underside of the bobcat's short tail is also white. A female shows her tail's white underside to signal her kittens. Bobcats are solitary animals and mark their territory to reduce encounters with other bobcats.

## HOW TO SPOT

**Size:** 1.5 to 2 feet (0.5 to 0.6 m) tall; 9 to 33 pounds (4 to 15 kg)

**North American Range:** Southern Canada to Mexico

**Habitat:** Forests, coastal swamps, deserts, and scrublands

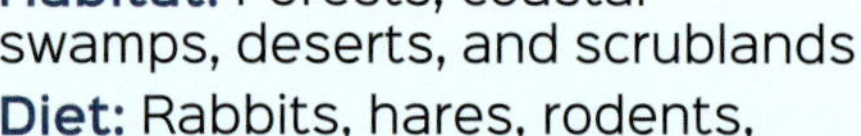

**Diet:** Rabbits, hares, rodents, and other small animals

# CANADA LYNX *(LYNX CANADENSIS)*

The Canada lynx has black ear tufts and a short tail with a black tip. It has large feet with furry pads, which help it walk across snow without sinking. The secretive lynx is about the size of a large house cat and avoids contact with humans. The lynx is solitary and often hunts at night. In the dark, it can spot its prey, usually rabbits, from 250 feet (76 m) away.

**Size:** Average 20 inches (51 cm) tall; 15 to 30 pounds (6.8 to 14 kg)

**North American Range:** Alaska, Canada, and northern United States

**Habitat:** Taiga and forests in the cold subarctic

**Diet:** Snowshoe hares, grouse, rodents, and other small animals

# COUGAR *(PUMA CONCOLOR)*

Cougars are sleek and graceful members of the cat family. They are also called mountain lions or pumas. Cougars have powerful hind legs that allow them to jump about 40 feet (12 m) horizontally or 18 feet (5.5 m) vertically. The cat's tawny-colored coat is darker along the back and lighter on the underside. Cougars usually hunt prey at dawn and dusk. They stalk, or quietly follow prey until they are close enough to pounce. Then the cats kill the prey by biting the head or neck. Cougars are solitary animals, and males roam large territories that often overlap with the territories of their mates. The cats seek shelter in caves, cracks in rocks, and thick brush.

Cub

## HOW TO SPOT

**Size:** 2.1 to 2.5 feet (0.6 to 0.8 m) tall; 75 to 158 pounds (34 to 72 kg)

**North American Range:** Southern Alaska to Panama

**Habitat:** Forests, swamps, deserts, and prairies

**Diet:** Deer, pigs, raccoons, armadillos, hares, squirrels, and other mammals

# JAGUAR *(PANTHERA ONCA)*

The jaguar is the largest cat in North America. Its size and strength make this cat the top predator where it lives. The jaguar's coat ranges from yellow or orange with black spots to solid black. Jaguars have large paws, which they use to swim and climb. Like many cats, jaguars have excellent night vision. They are solitary and mark their territory with waste or by clawing trees. When hunting at night, they surprise their prey and use their powerful jaws to pierce the prey's skull.

## HOW TO SPOT

**Size:** 2.2 to 2.4 feet (0.66 to 0.74 m) tall; 100 to 250 pounds (45 to 113 kg)

**North American Range:** Northern Mexico to Panama

**Habitat:** Tropical forests, swamps, grasslands, and deserts

**Diet:** Fish, turtles, caimans, deer, peccaries, capybaras, and other land animals

**FUN FACT**

The jaguar gets its name from the Tupí-Guaraní word *yaguar*, which means "he who kills with one leap."

# JAGUARUNDI

## *(HERPAILURUS YAGOUAROUNDI)*

The jaguarundi is a little bigger than a domestic cat. It has a long, thin body with short legs, a small, flattened head, and a long, tapered tail. Its coat is a solid reddish brown, brownish gray, or black. The jaguarundi moves quickly on the ground and can easily climb trees. It can even jump into the air to capture its prey. The cat lives alone. It is most active during the night. The jaguarundi has at least 13 different calls to communicate, including purrs, whistles, chatters, and chirps.

### HOW TO SPOT

**Size:** 10 to 14 inches (25 to 36 cm) tall; 6.6 to 15 pounds (3 to 6.8 kg)

**North American Range:** Northern Mexico to Panama

**Habitat:** Areas with dense ground cover in grasslands, swamps, woodlands, and forests

**Diet:** Small rodents, rabbits, armadillos, opossums, quail, wild turkeys, reptiles, frogs, and fish

# MARGAY *(LEOPARDUS WIEDII)*

The margay is a small cat with large eyes. Its fur ranges from gray to golden brown, and it has brown and black spots. On the cat's sides, the spots appear in various shapes. The cat's belly is white. The margay is a skilled climber and can hang from a branch by a single back foot. The margay is nocturnal and hunts in the tree canopy for prey at night. Its long tail provides balance, while its large eyes help it see in the dark.

## HOW TO SPOT

**Size:** 14 to 20 inches (36 to 51 cm) tall; 5 to 12 pounds (2.3 to 5.4 kg)

**North American Range:** Central Mexico through Panama

**Habitat:** Tropical and subtropical forests

**Diet:** Small mammals, birds, and reptiles

**FUN FACT**

The margay can rotate its hind legs 180 degrees, which allows it to climb headfirst down a tree trunk.

# OCELOT *(LEOPARDUS PARDALIS)*

The ocelot is a small- to medium-sized wildcat. Its coat features black spots and stripes on a tawny background. Ocelots live in places dense with plants. They sleep during the day in trees or bushes so predators can't spot them. They are active mainly at night and use their excellent sight and hearing to hunt. If an ocelot cannot finish eating its prey, it covers the carcass to keep it hidden until the cat is ready to eat again. Sometimes ocelots carry prey to a high branch to eat where fewer animals can steal the food.

## HOW TO SPOT

**Size:** 16 to 20 inches (41 to 51 cm) tall; 24 to 35 pounds (11 to 16 kg)

**North American Range:** Southern Texas and Arizona to Panama

**Habitat:** Areas with dense cover, including tropical forests, marshes, mangroves, and scrub

**Diet:** Small rodents, birds, and reptiles

**FUN FACT**
Every ocelot's coat pattern is unique.

# ONCILLA *(LEOPARDUS TIGRINUS)*

The oncilla is smaller and thinner than the similar margay and ocelot. Its muzzle is narrower. The oncilla has a thick, tawny coat with many dark spots. Its underbelly is lighter with dark spots. The backs of its ears are black with white spots, and its tail has several irregular rings. The oncilla's color pattern helps it blend into the irregular patches of sunlight and shade in its tropical forest habitat. This cat is primarily nocturnal and solitary. It is a skilled climber but usually hunts on the ground.

## HOW TO SPOT

**Size:** 8 to 10 inches (20 to 25 cm) tall; 3.3 to 6.6 pounds (1.5 to 3 kg)

**North American Range:** Costa Rica and Panama

**Habitat:** Forests, subtropical forests, savannas, and thorny scrub

**Diet:** Small mammals and reptiles

# NORTHERN RACCOON

## *(PROCYON LOTOR)*

The northern raccoon is a common mammal across North America. It has a sturdy body, a distinctive black mask, and a ringed tail. Its fur is typically gray and black with a lighter gray underbelly. Raccoons are active mainly at night. They usually leave their dens after dusk and return in the morning. They make their dens in places such as hollow trees, debris piles, or crawl spaces under houses. Raccoons are not picky eaters. They eat all types of plants and animals. They sometimes raid garbage cans and bird feeders in search of food.

## HOW TO SPOT

**Size:** 2 to 3 feet (0.6 to 0.9 m) long including tail; 10 to 30 pounds (4.5 to 14 kg)

**North American Range:** Southern Canada to Panama

**Habitat:** Deserts, tropical forests, hardwood forests, and urban areas

**Diet:** Fruits, acorns, seeds, bird and turtle eggs, insects, frogs, fish, and small mammals

# RINGTAIL *(BASSARISCUS ASTUTUS)*

The ringtail resembles a small fox or raccoon. Its long, bushy tail has black-and-white rings. White rings of fur surround its large eyes. The ringtail has a gray body, short legs, and large, round ears. Ringtails are good climbers. They make their dens in rocky hollows, where they spend most of the day sleeping. They are active at night, when they search for food. The ringtail's sharp eyesight helps it move around in the dark and spot food.

## HOW TO SPOT

**Size:** 1 to 1.5 feet (0.3 to 0.5 m) long including tail; 1 to 2 pounds (0.5 to 0.9 kg)

**North American Range:** Southwestern Oregon through southwestern United States and northern Mexico

**Habitat:** Dry, rocky habitats, deserts, woodlands, and coniferous forests

**Diet:** Fruits, insects, amphibians, reptiles, birds, bird eggs, and small mammals

# STRIPED SKUNK *(MEPHITIS MEPHITIS)*

The striped skunk is easily recognized by its black fur with a white V from the head down its body. Striped skunks have small ears and dark eyes. Their small head is triangular. When threatened, the skunk first hisses and stamps its feet. If the threat remains, the skunk shoots an oily, foul-smelling liquid from under its tail at the enemy. The skunk's spray is accurate up to ten feet (3 m) away.

## HOW TO SPOT

**Size:** 1.5 to 2.7 feet (0.5 to 0.8 m) long including tail; 1.5 to 13 pounds (0.7 to 5.9 kg)

**North American Range:** Southern Canada to northern Mexico

**Habitat:** Forests, woodlands, grasslands, agricultural fields, and urban areas

**Diet:** Insects, bird eggs, amphibians, small mammals, fish, and reptiles

**FUN FACT**

Young skunks walk single file behind their mother. They learn how to hunt and forage by watching her.

## WHITE-NOSED COATI

### *(NASUA NARICA)*

The white-nosed coati has a reddish-brown to black coat. Its belly is lighter. The coati's face has black-and-gray markings and white spots. The coati often holds its black-ringed tail erect for balance. The coati's strong claws and long snout help it dig and forage in narrow openings and holes for food. Adult males are solitary, while adult females live in groups called bands with other females and their young.

### HOW TO SPOT

**Size:** 2.6 to 4.3 feet (0.8 to 1.3 m) long including tail; 6.5 to 13 pounds (2.9 to 5.9 kg)

**North American Range:** Arizona through Panama

**Habitat:** Dry, open forests and tropical woodlands

**Diet:** Fruits, invertebrates, small rodents, and lizards

# AMERICAN BADGER *(TAXIDEA TAXUS)*

The American badger has a flat body and short legs. Its black or brown fur has white stripes on the cheeks and down the back of the head. The American badger uses its long claws to dig dens and burrows for sleeping, hunting, and storing food. This solitary badger is most active during the summer. It retreats to its den during the winter for days or weeks. The American badger's loose fur and thick neck muscles make it difficult for predators to grab. When threatened, the badger hisses, growls, and snarls. The badger also releases an unpleasant odor to deter predators. When attacked, it uses its long claws and teeth to fight.

**FUN FACT**

**When hunting, the badger digs its prey out of the prey's burrow.**

## HOW TO SPOT

**Size:** 1.7 to 2.9 feet (0.5 to 0.9 m) long including tail; 8 to 25 pounds (3.6 to 11 kg)

**North American Range:** Southwestern Canada, western and central United States, and northern mountain ranges in Mexico

**Habitat:** Open grasslands, pastures, and fields

**Diet:** Small mammals such as ground squirrels, rats, gophers, and mice

# AMERICAN MARTEN

## *(MARTES AMERICANA)*

The American marten is a small animal in the weasel family with a long body and short legs. It has rounded ears and black eyes. Its fur is yellowish brown with dark brown legs and tail. Its throat has yellowish-white fur. The solitary marten is primarily nocturnal. It leaps and zigzags along the forest floor. The marten's sharp, curved claws help it climb trees. The animal uses an odor to mark trees in its territory. It can walk on snow without sinking in thanks to its large, furry paws.

### HOW TO SPOT

**Size:** 21 to 26 inches (53 to 66 cm) long including tail; 2 to 4 pounds (0.9 to 1.8 kg)

**North American Range:** Northern regions from Alaska to northern New Mexico

**Habitat:** Dense forests and mountains

**Diet:** Pikas, chipmunks, squirrels, rabbits, insects, and berries

# AMERICAN MINK *(NEOGALE VISON)*

The American mink is a small predator in the weasel family with a long, thin body and short legs. It has a pointy face and a long tail. The mink is nocturnal and has excellent night vision. Its thick fur is covered with oils that make its coat waterproof. The mink has partially webbed toes that help it swim well and hunt for prey in the water. It kills prey by biting it on the neck. When threatened, the mink can spray a foul-smelling liquid. A very territorial animal, the mink also marks its territory with its scent to keep other mink away.

## HOW TO SPOT

**Size:** 1.5 to 2.3 feet (0.5 to 0.7 m) long including tail; 1.5 to 3.5 pounds (0.7 to 1.6 kg)

**North American Range:** Most of the United States and Canada

**Habitat:** Areas near rivers, streams, lakes, ponds, and marshes

**Diet:** Muskrats, rabbits, mice, chipmunks, fish, snakes, frogs, birds, and other small animals

## FUN FACT

A mink purrs like a cat when it is happy or content, and it hisses when it is upset.

# BLACK-FOOTED FERRET

## *(MUSTELA NIGRIPES)*

The black-footed ferret is a short, sleek mammal with yellowish-brown fur, a black mask on its face, black feet, and a tail with a black tip. The ferret has large front feet and claws that help it dig. It is nocturnal and spends most of the day underground in burrows. Ferrets use these burrows for sleeping, hunting prey, giving birth, and taking shelter from weather and predators. Ferrets come out at night to hunt and play. Ferrets are vocal and chatter, hiss, chortle, and whimper to communicate with each other. As solitary animals, ferrets typically live alone except during breeding season or when raising young.

### HOW TO SPOT

**Size:** 1.5 to 2 feet (0.5 to 0.6 m) long including tail; 1.5 to 2.5 pounds (0.7 to 1.1 kg)

**North American Range:** Montana, South Dakota, Wyoming, and Arizona

**Habitat:** Plains

**Diet:** Prairie dogs, mice, rats, ground squirrels, rabbits, birds, reptiles, and insects

# ERMINE *(MUSTELA ERMINEA)*

The ermine is a small but fierce member of the weasel family. It has a long, thin body with short legs and a triangular head. In summer, its fur is reddish brown. In winter, the ermine's fur turns completely white with a black-tipped tail. The ermine is a skilled hunter and can take down an adult rabbit with a bite at the base of the skull. Ermines investigate their environment, often standing on their hind legs and raising their head to look around. Ermines use their excellent senses of smell, eyesight, and hearing to find prey. They make dens in hollow logs, as well as stumps, roots, brush piles, or rocks.

Winter coat

## HOW TO SPOT

**Size:** 7 to 17 inches (18 to 43 cm) long including tail; 3.5 to 6.3 ounces (99 to 179 g)

**North American Range:** Alaska and Canada to northern United States

**Habitat:** Woodlands and marshes near rivers and streams; open areas near forests and shrublands

**Diet:** Small mammals, birds, amphibians, fish, eggs, and insects

Summer coat

# FISHER *(PEKANIA PENNANTI)*

The fisher is a member of the weasel family with a long, slim body. It has short legs and a long, tapered tail. Its dark-brown coat is thick and shiny. Fishers use their claws to climb trees, and they can jump from tree to tree. These mammals are active during the day and at night. They typically live alone except during mating season. Fishers use their sense of smell to hunt prey on the ground and in trees.

## HOW TO SPOT

**Size:** 2 to 2.5 feet (0.6 to 0.8 m) long including tail; 6 to 18 pounds (2.7 to 8.2 kg)

**North American Range:** Southern Canada, New England, New York, Pennsylvania, Virginia, and West Virginia

**Habitat:** Forests

**Diet:** Small animals, carrion, berries, and nuts

## HUNTING PORCUPINES

Fishers are among the few animals that hunt the prickly porcupine. The fisher uses its quickness and agility to circle the porcupine and avoid its quills and tail. As the porcupine tires, the fisher moves to strike the porcupine on its face, where it is not protected by quills. After repeated strikes, the fisher lands a deadly bite. The fisher turns over the dead porcupine and eats its belly, where there are no quills.

# LONG-TAILED WEASEL

## *(MUSTELA FRENATA)*

The long-tailed weasel has short legs and a long, slim body and neck. Its small head allows it to easily follow prey into underground burrows. The long-tailed weasel's fur is brown with a whitish-yellow underbelly. It has a long, black-tipped tail. In northern regions, the weasel's fur turns white in winter. The long-tailed weasel lives alone in burrows, in hollow logs, or under roots and rocks. It builds nests of grass, leaves, and fur. It moves mainly at night but is sometimes active during the day. Long-tailed weasels aggressively defend their territory. They puff up, scream, and bark to threaten other weasels entering their area.

### HOW TO SPOT

**Size:** 13 to 18 inches (33 to 46 cm) long including tail; 4.8 to 11 ounces (136 to 312 g)

**North American Range:** Southern Canada; most of United States, Mexico, and Central America

**Habitat:** Woodlands, open fields, farmlands, and forest edges

**Diet:** Voles, gophers, mice, squirrels, rabbits, birds, eggs, snakes, frogs, and insects

# NORTH AMERICAN RIVER OTTER *(LONTRA CANADENSIS)*

The North American river otter is a semiaquatic mammal. Its thick fur keeps it warm in cold water. The otter's webbed feet and strong tail help it swim fast. River otters can hold their breath up to eight minutes to stay underwater. The waters where they live can be murky, so the otters use their long whiskers to find prey. Claws help them grip slippery prey. River otters are social animals. They play and slide in snow, mud, and water. Their playful activities help otters bond and give them hunting practice.

## HOW TO SPOT

**Size:** 2.5 to 5 feet (0.8 to 1.5 m) long, including tail; 10 to 33 pounds (4.5 to 15 kg)

**North American Range:** Most of Canada, United States, and Colorado and Rio Grande delta areas in Mexico

**Habitat:** Areas near streams, rivers, lakes, ponds, and marshes

**Diet:** Fish, frogs, turtles, crayfish, insects, and small mammals

# SEA OTTER *(ENHYDRA LUTRIS)*

The sea otter is the largest member of the weasel family. It is aquatic, living mostly in the ocean. Webbed feet help these mammals swim, and their fur repels water. Their nostrils and ears can close to keep out water. Sea otters are often spotted floating on their back in the water, frequently in groups. They can even sleep while floating. Sea otters have a thick undercoat that traps air to create insulation against cold water. After eating, sea otters carefully clean their coat in the ocean. Female otters give birth in the water and nurse while floating on their back. Mothers teach their young to swim and hunt.

## HOW TO SPOT

**Size:** 3.3 to 4.9 feet (1 to 1.5 m) long, including tail; 31 to 99 pounds (14 to 45 kg)

**North American Range:** The Pacific coast

**Habitat:** Coastal waters usually less than one-half mile (0.8 km) from shore

**Diet:** Shellfish, sea urchins, crabs, squid, octopuses, fish, and other aquatic animals

# WOLVERINE *(GULO GULO)*

The wolverine is the largest land-dwelling member of the weasel family. It has brownish-black fur and long claws and teeth. When threatened, a wolverine produces a stinky spray to scare off predators. Its broad paws and sharp claws help it move across deep snow and slippery ice. The wolverine can run up to 30 miles per hour (48 kmh) in pursuit of prey. It also jumps from trees onto prey. Once it kills the prey, the wolverine buries food to eat later. It keeps other animals from eating the stored food by spraying it with a smelly musk. The wolverine also eats carrion.

## HOW TO SPOT

**Size:** 2.8 to 4.6 feet (0.9 to 1.4 m) long including tail; 20 to 66 pounds (9.1 to 30 kg)

**North American Range:** Arctic and subarctic regions of North America

**Habitat:** Grasslands, alpine forests, taiga, boreal forests, and tundra

**Diet:** Deer, moose, wild sheep, elk, and smaller mammals such as rabbits, beavers, and squirrels

# AMERICAN BLACK BEAR

## *(URSUS AMERICANUS)*

The American black bear is the most common bear in North America. It is often spotted in forests. These bears are skilled tree climbers. Their fur ranges from bluish black and brown to cinnamon. Black bears eat many foods, including grasses, berries, fish, and other mammals. They even eat human food and garbage from campsites. The black bear roams a large territory alone. It makes dens in caves, burrows, and other sheltered areas. In summer and fall, the bear eats a lot of food, building up its body fat. It uses this store of fat to survive the winter season while it is dormant in its den. Females give birth to two or three cubs every two years. The cubs stay with their mother for about two years.

### HOW TO SPOT

**Size:** 2 to 3 feet (0.6 to 0.9 m) tall; 200 to 600 pounds (91 to 272 kg)

**North American Range:** Canada, United States, and northern Mexico

**Habitat:** Forests and open alpine areas

**Diet:** Many plants and animals

## BROWN BEAR *(URSUS ARCTOS)*

The brown bear is a large bear that lives in the northern regions of North America. The bear's fur is usually dark brown but can range from light tan to almost black. Brown bears are strong and can be dangerous, though attacks on humans are rare. They run as fast as a horse and are good swimmers. The brown bear has a large, muscular shoulder hump for digging. It uses its long claws to dig and to catch prey. Brown bears are omnivores, eating both plants and animals.

### HOW TO SPOT

**Size:** 3 to 5 feet (0.9 to 1.5 m) tall; 176 to 1,320 pounds (80 to 600 kg)

**North American Range:** Alaska and western Canada

**Habitat:** Forests, mountains, tundra, and coastlines

**Diet:** Fruits and other plant material, insects, birds, fish, and mammals

### HIBERNATION

Several bear species, including brown bears and black bears, hibernate in winter when food is scarce. As the bears settle in their dens, their heart rate and breathing slow. They use the body fat stored in summer for energy. When hibernating, bears go for weeks without eating, drinking, urinating, or defecating.

# GRIZZLY BEAR

## *(URSUS ARCTOS HORRIBILIS)*

Grizzly bears are a subspecies of brown bear. They are large bears, and their fur is light tan to dark brown. The bear's coat has a dense undercoat covered by longer guard hairs tipped in silver or gold. This gives the bear the grizzled appearance that led to its name. The grizzly bear has a large shoulder hump that holds muscles that power the bear's digging. The bear has long claws on its front feet, which help it dig dens and search for food. Adult grizzly bears live alone except during mating season and when females are raising their young. However, their home ranges often overlap with those of other grizzlies.

### HOW TO SPOT

**Size:** 3 to 4 feet (0.9 to 1.2 m) tall; 210 to 860 pounds (95 to 390 kg)

**North American Range:** Alaska, western Canada, Washington, Idaho, Montana, Wyoming, and Colorado

**Habitat:** Woodlands, forests, alpine meadows, and prairies

**Diet:** Insects, berries, nuts, roots, fish, mammals, carrion, and more

## POLAR BEAR *(URSUS MARITIMUS)*

The polar bear is the largest bear in the world. It lives in the cold Arctic and spends most of its life in the ocean or on sea ice. Polar bears are strong swimmers, moving about six miles per hour (9.7 kmh) through the water. They paddle with their front paws and use their hind legs to steer. A thick layer of body fat and a water-repellent white coat protect them from the cold air and water. Polar bears spend more than half of their time on the hunt for food, mainly seals. A polar bear waits for a seal to come to the surface near a hole in the ice to breathe. Then the polar bear grabs the seal, dragging it onto the ice.

### HOW TO SPOT

**Size:** 3.3 to 5 feet (1 to 1.5 m) tall; 300 to 1,300 pounds (136 to 590 kg)

**North American Range:** Arctic Circle to the North Pole and the Arctic Ocean

**Habitat:** Ocean, sea ice, and adjacent coastal areas

**Diet:** Ringed seals, bearded seals, and other polar animals

# BIG BROWN BAT *(EPTESICUS FUSCUS)*

The big brown bat is found in almost every part of North America. These bats live in colonies under loose bark and in small cavities in trees. They roost in buildings and under bridges. Big brown bats have brown to copper fur on their back with lighter belly fur. Their black ears are small and round. They also have black wing membranes and a black tail. Big brown bats are among the fastest bat species, flying up to 40 miles per hour (64 kmh). They hibernate in caves, mines, attics, or other sheltered locations during the winter.

## HOW TO SPOT

**Size:** Wingspan 12 to 16 inches (30 to 41 cm); 0.5 to 1.2 ounces (14 to 34 g)

**North American Range:** Most of North America

**Habitat:** Deserts, meadows, cities, forests, mountains, and scrub

**Diet:** Insects, especially beetles

# EASTERN RED BAT

## *(LASIURUS BOREALIS)*

The eastern red bat is the most common tree bat in North America. It is a medium-sized bat. Males are bright red while females and young have muted colors. Both males and females may have white-tipped hairs and white fur patches on their shoulders and wrists. Eastern red bats usually live alone but gather to mate. They also join groups when migrating to hibernate in warmer areas. These bats are fast flyers and hunt for food at night.

### HOW TO SPOT

**Size:** Wingspan 11 to 13 inches (28 to 33 cm); 0.4 to 0.6 ounces (11 to 17 g)

**North American Range:** West Coast from southern Canada to northern Mexico

**Habitat:** Forests, forest edges, and hedgerows

**Diet:** Beetles, moths, ants, flies, and other insects

# LITTLE BROWN BAT

## *(MYOTIS LUCIFUGUS)*

The little brown bat ranges in color from brown to golden. As with all bats, a membrane connected to long finger bones forms the little brown bat's wings. These bats live in colonies numbering in the hundreds of thousands. They gather at nesting sites called roosts, which can be in buildings, caves, trees, rocks, or woodpiles. Little brown bats hibernate in caves and similar places during winter. A female bat usually has a single pup. After one month, the young bat can fly and hunt.

### HOW TO SPOT

**Size:** Wingspan 8 to 11 inches (20 to 28 cm); 0.2 to 0.5 ounces (6 to 14 g)

**North American Range:** Canada, northern United States, and high-elevation forests in Mexico

**Habitat:** Forests, caves, mines, and buildings

**Diet:** Flies, gnats, moths, wasps, beetles, and other insects

### ECHOLOCATION

Most bats use echolocation to find prey and navigate in the dark. Echolocation is like the sonar used on ships. The bat releases pulses of high-frequency sound. The sound travels through the air and bounces off objects in its path. The bat listens to the returning echo sound to determine the size, shape, and distance of nearby objects.

# MEXICAN FREE-TAILED BAT

## *(TADARIDA BRASILIENSIS)*

The Mexican free-tailed bat is medium-sized with reddish-brown to dark-brown fur. These bats have black ears and wrinkled lips. They have long tails that stretch beyond the tail membrane, giving them their name. The bats also have long, narrow wings. As winter approaches, Mexican free-tailed bats typically migrate south to Mexico and Central America. They roost in caves, under bridges, or in buildings.

### HOW TO SPOT

**Size:** Wingspan 12 to 14 inches (30 to 36 cm); 0.4 to 0.5 ounces (11 to 14 g)

**North American Range:** Western United States, south through Central America

**Habitat:** Caves, abandoned buildings, attics, and other shelters near water

**Diet:** Moths and other insects

# AMERICAN PIKA *(OCHOTONA PRINCEPS)*

American pikas are small mammals with round bodies that live in cold, rocky regions. They have thick brown fur to keep them warm. Their dark fur helps them blend into their rocky environment. Furry paws keep them from slipping on snow. Pikas have rounded ears. Their fur hides a short tail. These animals are active during the day and spend much of their time looking for food, some of which they store in dens for winter. Pikas use rock piles and other rocky areas to build dens. They live in colonies and give warning calls to alert other pikas when predators are nearby.

## HOW TO SPOT

**Size:** 6 to 8 inches (15 to 20 cm) long; 5 to 6 ounces (142 to 170 g)

**North American Range:** Western North America from British Columbia to New Mexico

**Habitat:** Alpine and subalpine areas

**Diet:** Grasses, thistles, wildflowers, and other plants

# ARCTIC HARE *(LEPUS ARCTICUS)*

The Arctic hare is North America's largest hare. It has thick white fur that provides warmth and camouflage in the snow. In the spring, the hare's fur turns bluish gray to blend into rocks and vegetation. The speedy Arctic hare runs up to 40 miles per hour (64 kmh). The hares often gather in groups of dozens to hundreds. They sometimes dig shelters in the snow and huddle together to keep warm in the cold.

Winter coat

## HOW TO SPOT

**Size:** 19 to 26 inches (48 to 66 cm) long; 6 to 15 pounds (2.7 to 6.8 kg)

**North American Range:** Northern Canada

**Habitat:** Tundra and rocky mountains

**Diet:** Woody plants, mosses, sedges, roots, and berries

Summer coat

# BLACK-TAILED JACKRABBIT

## *(LEPUS CALIFORNICUS)*

The black-tailed jackrabbit is a large rabbit found in open grasslands and desert scrub areas of western North America. It is recognized by its long, black-tipped ears. The jackrabbit's ears help it release heat to cool its body temperature. Large eyes that sit high and toward the sides of the head allow the jackrabbit to see a wide area and spot predators. During the day, the jackrabbit digs a shallow depression in the ground to rest. It comes out at dusk and is active throughout the night, foraging for food. Jackrabbits can run 40 miles per hour (64 kmh) and use their speed to escape predators.

### HOW TO SPOT

**Size:** 18 to 25 inches (46 to 64 cm) long; 3 to 7 pounds (1.4 to 3.2 kg)

**North American Range:** West-central and western United States to Baja California and south-central Mexico

**Habitat:** Brushlands, prairies, and meadows

**Diet:** Grasses, leaves, clover, twigs, cacti, and other plants

# EASTERN COTTONTAIL

## *(SYLVILAGUS FLORIDANUS)*

The eastern cottontail rabbit is known for its white tail, which looks much like a cotton ball. The rabbit's fur varies from reddish brown to gray with a white underside. Cottontail rabbits typically hide in vegetation during the day and come out to eat at night. They feed on plants such as grasses and herbs. When a cottontail senses a predator, the rabbit escapes in a zigzag pattern, running up to 18 miles per hour (29 kmh). Females dig nests into the ground and give birth to three to eight helpless babies three to four times per year. In four to five weeks, the young rabbits can live on their own.

### HOW TO SPOT

**Size:** 16 to 19 inches (41 to 48 cm) long; 2 to 3 pounds (0.9 to 1.4 kg)

**North American Range:** Southern Canada to Panama, from the East Coast to the Great Plains

**Habitat:** Edges of open spaces such as fields, farms, and meadows

**Diet:** Grasses, herbs, garden plants, lettuce, bark, twigs, buds, and other vegetation

# PYGMY RABBIT

## *(BRACHYLAGUS IDAHOENSIS)*

The pygmy rabbit is North America's smallest rabbit. Its coat ranges from brown to dark gray. White fur lines the edges of its short ears. Unlike other North American rabbits, pygmy rabbits do not have white on their tail. They live in areas with tall, dense sagebrush, which provides them shelter and food. Pygmy rabbits dig burrows in loose soil. These burrows provide shelter and protection from predators such as coyotes, hawks, and owls.

### HOW TO SPOT

**Size:** 9 to 12 inches (23 to 30 cm) long; 0.8 to 1 pound (0.4 to 0.5 kg)

**North American Range:** Washington, Oregon, Idaho, Montana, Wyoming, California, Nevada, and Utah

**Habitat:** Areas with tall, dense sagebrush

**Diet:** Sagebrush, grasses

# SNOWSHOE HARE

## *(LEPUS AMERICANUS)*

The snowshoe hare changes color with the seasons. It is white in winter, making it hard to spot in the snow. In spring and summer, its fur becomes reddish brown, camouflaging it against rocks and soil. The tips of the hare's ears remain black all year long. The snowshoe hare has large hind legs with thick fur and large toes, which act similar to a pair of snowshoes as the hare walks on top of the snow. These hares come out at night to feed and are most often active at dawn and dusk. When young hares hear a predator, they freeze to blend into their environment. Older hares use their speed to escape.

### HOW TO SPOT

**Size:** 18 to 20 inches (46 to 51 cm) long; 3 to 4 pounds (1.4 to 1.8 kg)

**North American Range:** Canada and the US Rocky and Appalachian Mountains

**Habitat:** Coniferous and boreal forests

**Diet:** Grasses, flowers, new tree growth, and other plants

Winter coat

Summer coat

### HARES VS. RABBITS

Hares and rabbits have differences. Hares are typically larger, with bigger ears and longer legs. When danger gets too close, hares use their long legs and big feet to run away. Rabbits usually freeze and attempt to blend into their environment. When born, hares have fur and are ready to run, while newborn rabbits are helpless.

# AMERICAN BEAVER

## *(CASTOR CANADENSIS)*

The American beaver is North America's largest rodent. This brown, semiaquatic mammal lives mostly in the water. Its distinctive long, flat tail helps it swim quickly and can also be slapped on the water to sound an alarm. The beaver has waterproof fur to keep it warm and dry and webbed feet to help it swim. Beavers use branches and mud to build shelters called lodges. The lodge entrance is usually underwater. Beavers mate for life. Females have one litter of kits each year.

**FUN FACT**

A beaver's teeth never stop growing. It chews on wood to keep its teeth filed down.

### HOW TO SPOT

**Size:** 3 to 4 feet (0.9 to 1.2 m) long including tail; 35 to 65 pounds (16 to 29 kg)

**North American Range:** Canada, United States, and northern Mexico

**Habitat:** Ponds, lakes, rivers, and streams

**Diet:** Trees, shrubs, and other plant material

# AMERICAN RED SQUIRREL

## *(TAMIASCIURUS HUDSONICUS)*

The American red squirrel is a small, tree-dwelling rodent. It has reddish-brown fur, a white underbelly, and a bushy tail. The squirrel's black eyes are ringed with white fur. The red squirrel collects seeds and nuts in the summer and stores them for winter. The squirrel often forgets to dig up some of its seeds, and new trees then grow. The red squirrel is territorial and chatters loudly at intruders.

### HOW TO SPOT

**Size:** 11 to 15 inches (28 to 38 cm) long including tail; 6 to 7 ounces (170 to 198 g)

**North American Range:** Alaska, Canada, Rocky Mountains, and eastern United States

**Habitat:** Coniferous and mixed forests

**Diet:** Coniferous tree seeds and cones, bird eggs, berries, and fruits

# BLACK RAT *(RATTUS RATTUS)*

The black rat is a medium-sized rat with large ears. Its tail, which has very little fur, is longer than its body. The rat is mainly black with a lighter underbelly. Black rats are skilled climbers and often build nests in trees, roofs, and other high places. The rats are most active at dusk and hunt at night. As social animals, black rats typically live in clans of dozens of individuals. A clan is led by a single male and a few females. The females defend the clan's territory aggressively. Black rats can be destructive where they live, stripping bark off trees and contaminating human food sources with urine and droppings.

## HOW TO SPOT

**Size:** 10 to 12 inches (25 to 30 cm) long including tail; 2.5 to 11 ounces (71 to 312 g)

**North American Range:** Throughout North America, especially coastal areas

**Habitat:** Buildings in urban and rural areas—especially ports and shipyards—and coastal forests

**Diet:** Fruits, grains, cereals, seeds, leaves, bark, and other vegetation

## CARRYING DISEASE

Rats and other rodents can carry and transmit pathogens that cause human disease. Humans can become infected by handling rats, being bitten, or eating food contaminated with rat feces, urine, or saliva. Rats can also have fleas or ticks that become infected and spread disease to humans.

# BROWN LEMMING

## *(LEMMUS TRIMUCRONATUS)*

The brown lemming is a small rodent with a round body, brown fur, and a short tail. The lemming's face is flat with small eyes and ears partially hidden by thick fur. Brown lemmings are solitary animals that live alone in burrows. They dig under the snow to keep warm. They defend their territory and avoid other lemmings except when mating. Brown lemmings eat live plant parts, such as fresh grasses and mosses. In winter, they look under the snow for food.

### HOW TO SPOT

**Size:** 4.9 to 5.1 inches (12.5 to 13 cm) long including tail; 2 to 2.4 ounces (58 to 68 g)

**North American Range:** Alaska and Canada

**Habitat:** Tundra

**Diet:** Sedges, grasses, and other plant material

# BUSHY-TAILED WOODRAT

## *(NEOTOMA CINEREA)*

The bushy-tailed woodrat is one of the largest and most common woodrats. It is a medium-sized rodent ranging in color from light brown to gray. The woodrat has a white underside. It gets its name from its long, bushy tail. Also called a pack rat, the woodrat collects objects that it finds interesting, such as sticks, bones, pieces of rope, and feathers. The rat brings these items back to its nest, where it marks the items with its scent by urinating on them.

### HOW TO SPOT

**Size:** 13 to 17 inches (33 to 43 cm) long including tail; 7 to 21 ounces (198 to 595 g)

**North American Range:** Western North America from Arctic Canada to northern New Mexico and Arizona

**Habitat:** Caves, rockslides, cracks in rocks, and sometimes abandoned buildings

**Diet:** Pine needles and pine cones, leaves, fungi, fruits, and other plant parts

# CALIFORNIA GROUND SQUIRREL

## *(OTOSPERMOPHILUS BEECHEYI)*

The California ground squirrel is grayish brown with white speckles. It has a bushy tail. White fur lines its eyes. Strong claws help it dig burrow systems. These squirrels stay close to their burrows, which sometimes house other California ground squirrels. Each squirrel has its own entrance. The California ground squirrel hides in its burrow to escape predators. It spends time outside sunning itself.

### HOW TO SPOT

**Size:** 18 to 29 inches (46 to 74 cm) long including tail; 10 to 26 ounces (280 to 738 g)

**North American Range:** Southwestern Washington, western Oregon, California, western Nevada, and Baja California, Mexico

**Habitat:** Grasslands, oak woodlands, and pastures with loose soil

**Diet:** Seeds, fruits, eggs, and insects

# DEER MOUSE

## *(PEROMYSCUS MANICULATUS)*

The deer mouse is the most common mammal in North America. It is a small rodent with large black eyes, big ears, long whiskers, and a tail. The mouse's color ranges from grayish to reddish brown with a lighter underbelly and white feet. Deer mice are mainly nocturnal and come out at night to gather food. They stay mostly on the ground but can climb too. They build nests of plant matter near the ground in stumps, logs, burrows, brush piles, and other similar spots. They often live in small groups and huddle together in nests to keep warm in winter.

### HOW TO SPOT

**Size:** 4.4 to 8 inches (11.2 to 20 cm) long including tail; 0.35 to 0.85 ounces (10 to 24 g)

**North American Range:** Alaska, Canada, and United States to central Mexico

**Habitat:** Pastures, meadows, prairies, and fields

**Diet:** Insects, nuts, seeds, grains, fruits, and some vegetation

# EASTERN CHIPMUNK

## *(TAMIAS STRIATUS)*

The eastern chipmunk is a small rodent with reddish-brown fur, black stripes, and a white underbelly. Its tail provides balance when climbing trees. The chipmunk spends most of its day gathering food. It makes a "chip-chip" sound as it gathers nuts, acorns, and seeds. The eastern chipmunk carries and stores its food in its cheek pouches, which can stretch three times bigger than their usual size. In winter, the chipmunk sleeps in its den. It wakes every few weeks to eat its stored food.

### HOW TO SPOT

**Size:** 7.3 to 12 inches (19 to 30 cm) long including tail; 2.3 to 5.3 ounces (65 to 150 g)

**North American Range:** Southeastern Canada and eastern United States

**Habitat:** Open deciduous forests and edges of woodlands

**Diet:** Nuts, acorns, seeds, mushrooms, fruits, berries, corn, insects, bird eggs, and snails

# EASTERN FOX SQUIRREL

## *(SCIURUS NIGER)*

The eastern fox squirrel is the largest species of tree squirrel in North America. It has rusty-brown fur and a bushy tail. Its powerful back legs help the squirrel jump through the branches. Fox squirrels have excellent vision, hearing, and smell. They communicate by barking, chattering, screaming, and whining. To threaten another squirrel, the fox squirrel stands up, flicking its tail over its back.

### HOW TO SPOT

**Size:** 19 to 29 inches (48 to 74 cm) long including tail; 1 to 3 pounds (0.5 to 1.4 kg)

**North American Range:** Southeastern and south-central Canada to northern Mexico

**Habitat:** Deciduous and mixed forest

**Diet:** Leaves, seeds, grains, nuts, insects, and small birds and mammals

# EASTERN GRAY SQUIRREL

## *(SCIURUS CAROLINENSIS)*

The eastern gray squirrel has gray fur with some reddish-brown patches. The squirrel's long, bushy tail provides balance when moving in trees. The gray squirrel takes shelter in holes in trees. When angry or scared, it makes a chirping or chattering sound. Eastern gray squirrels collect nuts, acorns, and seeds and bury them underground to eat later. The squirrel uses its bushy tail as a blanket when it's cold. It does not hibernate in winter but does become less active.

**FUN FACT**

Gray squirrels pretend to bury nuts and acorns to trick other squirrels and prevent them from stealing their food.

## HOW TO SPOT

**Size:** 16 to 20 inches (41 to 51 cm) long including tail; 12 to 26.5 ounces (340 to 750 g)

**North American Range:** Canada into eastern and midwestern United States

**Habitat:** Hardwood forests and other wooded areas

**Diet:** Acorns, walnuts, seeds, fungi, and elm buds

# GROUNDHOG *(MARMOTA MONAX)*

The groundhog is also called a woodchuck. This common rodent has a heavy body with short, powerful legs and a short, fluffy tail. The groundhog's fur is brownish and grizzled. When startled, groundhogs make a shrill whistle call. Groundhogs dig burrows in slopes or banks near the edges of woodlands. A burrow usually has multiple entrances. During the day, groundhogs hunt for food or relax in the sun near the burrow entrance. Although they eat primarily native grasses and flowering plants, groundhogs that live near humans sometimes raid vegetable gardens. In winter, groundhogs hibernate in their burrows.

## HOW TO SPOT

**Size:** 20 to 34 inches (51 to 86 cm) long including tail; 4 to 14 pounds (1.8 to 6.4 kg)

**North American Range:** Alaska, Canada, and eastern and central United States

**Habitat:** Fields, meadows, woodland clearings, and urban and suburban yards

**Diet:** Grasses, flowering plants, clover, alfalfa, garden crops, and other plants

## GROUNDHOG DAY

German immigrants brought the tradition of using rodents to predict the weather to the United States. In 1877 the first Groundhog Day celebration was held in Punxsutawney, Pennsylvania. According to legend, if the groundhog comes out of its burrow on February 2 and sees its shadow, there will be six more weeks of winter. Spring will come early if the groundhog does not see its shadow.

## HOUSE MOUSE *(MUS MUSCULUS)*

The house mouse is a small rodent with a pointed nose and large, rounded ears. Its long tail is nearly hairless. Its fur ranges from light brown to black with a lighter underbelly. House mice have strong hearing, sight, and smell. Their whiskers help them feel surfaces and air movement. The mice often live in underground burrows or in cracks in rocks or walls. They build nests from soft materials such as paper and rags. Most house mice are nocturnal but can be active during the day. They run fast and are skilled climbers and jumpers.

### FUN FACT

Male mice can sing and change the notes in their song. However, their song is too high a frequency for humans to hear.

### HOW TO SPOT

**Size:** 4.9 to 7.9 inches (12.5 to 20 cm) long including tail; 0.4 to 1 ounce (11 to 28 g)

**North American Range:** Across North America

**Habitat:** Places near humans, such as houses, barns, fields, and other buildings

**Diet:** Leaves, roots, seeds, grains, nuts, fruits, insects, carrion, and arthropods

# MEADOW VOLE

## *(MICROTUS PENNSYLVANICUS)*

Meadow voles are small, stocky rodents. Compared with mice, their tails are short. An adult vole is a blend of brown and black and has a dark gray underbelly. Voles have rounded noses and chisel-shaped front teeth. These rodents dig many tunnels and burrows with multiple entrances. Several adult voles and their young can live in a single burrow system. Inside burrows, voles build nests with dry grass. Females place young pups in nests after birth. They nurse and protect their young until the pups are weaned at about 12 to 14 days old.

### HOW TO SPOT

**Size:** 5.5 to 7.7 inches (14 to 19.6 cm) long including tail; 1.2 to 1.8 ounces (34 to 51 g)

**North American Range:** Canada, United States, and northern Mexico

**Habitat:** Grassy areas such as grasslands, fields, and marshes

**Diet:** Leaves, roots, wood, bark, seeds, grains, nuts, fruits, and insects

# MUSKRAT *(ONDATRA ZIBETHICUS)*

Muskrats are large, semiaquatic rodents with reddish-brown fur and a long, nearly hairless tail. The muskrat has a rounded body, short legs, and barely visible ears. Muskrats live in wet environments, especially marshes. They dig burrows in waterway banks and build nests from piles of vegetation. Their partially webbed feet help them swim. These rodents can hold their breath underwater for 15 to 20 minutes. Muskrats live in large family groups within a territory. They communicate with a musky odor, which they also spread in their territory to keep away intruders.

## HOW TO SPOT

**Size:** 16 to 24 inches (41 to 61 cm) long including tail; 2 to 5 pounds (0.9 to 2.3 kg)

**North American Range:** Alaska and Canada to northern Mexico

**Habitat:** Marshes, ponds, lakes, and swamps

**Diet:** Cattails, sedges, other aquatic plants, crayfish, snails, and small fish

# NORTH AMERICAN PORCUPINE

## *(ERETHIZON DORSATUM)*

The North American porcupine is a large rodent. It is known for its many sharp quills. About 30,000 quills cover its body. When a predator approaches, the porcupine raises its quills and turns its back to the threat. The porcupine does not shoot its quills. Instead, when a predator gets too close, the quills pierce the predator's skin. The quills are lightly attached to the porcupine, so they pull away easily. Porcupines live mostly on the ground, but they can also climb trees and swim. Their orange tooth enamel contains iron, which helps make the teeth strong enough to chew wood.

### HOW TO SPOT

**Size:** 2 to 3 feet (0.6 to 0.9 m) long including tail; 11 to 31 pounds (5 to 14 kg)

**North American Range:** Canada, United States, and northern Mexico

**Habitat:** Forests, grasslands, desert shrub, and tundra

**Diet:** Tree bark, needles, berries, seeds, grasses, leaves, roots, stems, and other plant material

# POCKET GOPHER *(FAMILY GEOMYIDAE)*

Pocket gophers are medium-sized rodents known for their fur-lined cheek pockets. More than 30 species of pocket gophers live in North America. These gophers use their cheek pockets to carry food. Gophers are built for burrowing. They have large claws on their front paws and sensitive whiskers that help them sense movement in the dark. When digging, they cut roots and break apart soil with their large front teeth. Pocket gophers move large amounts of soil when digging tunnels, which helps aerate the soil, or loosen it so air and water can enter. The gophers typically live alone except during mating season. Females give birth in underground nest chambers. They care for their young for several weeks until the young can survive on their own.

**FUN FACT**

**A pocket gopher can push one short ton (0.9 metric tons) of soil aboveground per year.**

## HOW TO SPOT

**Size:** 5 to 14 inches (12.7 to 36 cm); up to 1 pound (0.5 kg)

**North American Range:** Canada to Panama

**Habitat:** Loose, sandy soil with edible plants

**Diet:** Roots, bulbs, stems, leaves, and other vegetation

# PRAIRIE DOG *(GENUS CYNOMYS)*

Prairie dogs are burrowing rodents and members of the squirrel family. They are known for digging complex burrows with multiple entrances and chambers. These large underground communities are called towns. Prairie dogs are social animals. Within a large colony, prairie dogs live in smaller family groups. A family group typically includes a male, a few females, and their young. Family groups play, share food, and groom each other. When they sense danger, prairie dogs warn each other with loud cries.

## HOW TO SPOT

**Size:** 12 to 15 inches (30 to 38 cm) long; 2 to 4 pounds (0.9 to 1.8 kg)

**North American Range:** Great Plains

**Habitat:** Prairies and open grasslands

**Diet:** Grasses, roots, and seeds

# ROCK SQUIRREL

## *(OTOSPERMOPHILUS VARIEGATUS)*

The rock squirrel is one of the largest squirrels. It has a speckled grayish-brown coat with a buff-white underside and a long, bushy tail. Rock squirrels are active during the day, particularly in the early morning and late afternoon. They are ground squirrels, but they can also climb trees to gather food. Sharp claws and strong legs help these squirrels dig burrows for shelter and food storage. They hide the burrow entrances under rocks. Rock squirrels are social and live in colonies of several squirrels.

### HOW TO SPOT

**Size:** 18 to 20 inches (46 to 51 cm) long including tail; 1.3 to 2 pounds (0.6 to 0.9 kg)

**North American Range:** Southwestern United States and Mexico

**Habitat:** Cliffs, canyon walls, boulder piles, and other rocky areas

**Diet:** Seeds, insects, beans, fruits, carrion, small birds, and eggs

# SOUTHERN FLYING SQUIRREL

## *(GLAUCOMYS VOLANS)*

The southern flying squirrel is one of two flying squirrel species in North America. Its fur is grayish brown, and it has a white belly. Flying squirrels do not actually fly. Instead, they glide. A flying squirrel leaps from a tree branch. It stretches a membrane between its front and back legs to glide to another tree. It moves its legs to steer and uses its tail as a brake. The flying squirrel can glide more than 150 feet (46 m). The squirrel nests in woodpecker holes, nest boxes, and other animals' abandoned nests.

### HOW TO SPOT

**Size:** 11.8 to 14.6 inches (30 to 37 cm) long including tail; 1.7 to 2.6 ounces (48 to 74 g)

**North American Range:** Eastern to central United States

**Habitat:** Deciduous and coniferous forests and woodlands

**Diet:** Seeds, nuts, fungi, fruits, insects, eggs, birds, and carrion

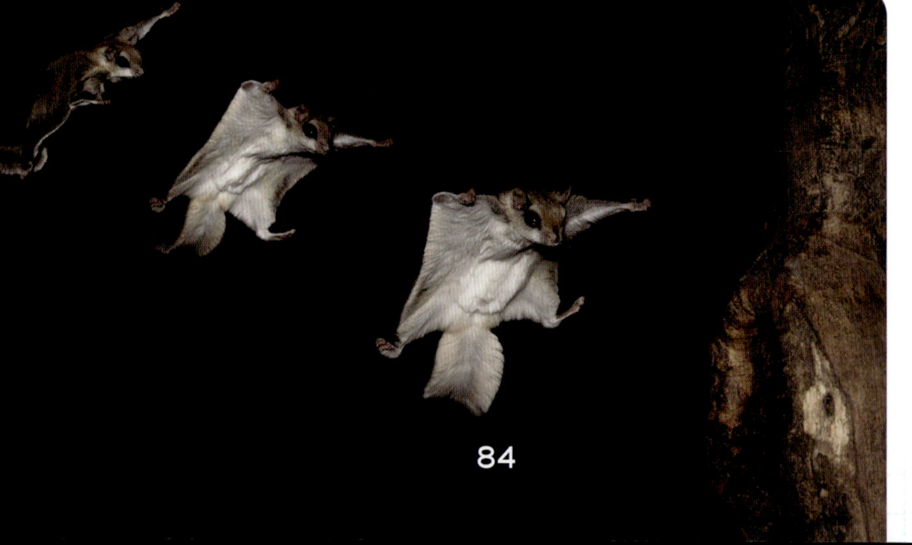

# YELLOW-BELLIED MARMOT

## *(MARMOTA FLAVIVENTRIS)*

The yellow-bellied marmot is a large rodent with a heavy body, small eyes, and round ears. The marmot's thick, powerful legs carry it across rough terrain and steep, rocky ground. The marmot is active mainly during the day, when it looks for food and grooms and suns itself. Marmots spend most of their time on the ground but sometimes climb trees. The marmot hibernates in a burrow for several months in winter. When predators are nearby, the marmot whistles, chucks, and trills to alert others of danger.

### FUN FACT

**Yellow-bellied marmots spend nearly half the year in hibernation, often huddled together with other marmots to save energy.**

### HOW TO SPOT

**Size:** 1.5 to 2 feet (0.5 to 0.6 m) long including tail; 4 to 12 pounds (1.8 to 5.4 kg)

**North American Range:** Southwestern Canada and western United States

**Habitat:** Steppes, alpine meadows, pastures, fields, and forest edges

**Diet:** Grasses, herbs, and flower seeds

# AMERICAN PYGMY SHREW

## *(SOREX HOYI)*

The American pygmy shrew is North America's smallest mammal. It has grayish-brown fur, a narrow head, and a pointed nose with whiskers. The American pygmy shrew spends most of its life foraging for food. It must eat three times its body weight per day. To do this, the shrew must catch prey every 15 to 30 minutes through the day and night. The shrew sleeps just a few minutes at a time.

### HOW TO SPOT

**Size:** 1.5 to 2 inches (3.8 to 5.1 cm) long excluding tail; 0.07 to 0.14 ounces (2 to 4 g)

**North American Range:** Alaska, Canada; Appalachian and US Rocky Mountains

**Habitat:** Forests, swamps, grassy clearings, bogs, and floodplains

**Diet:** Insects, including ants, flies, spiders, beetles, earthworms, grubs, and caterpillars

# EASTERN MOLE *(SCALOPUS AQUATICUS)*

The eastern mole is a small mammal with soft gray fur and a short tail. The mole has large webbed front feet. It digs with its large claws. The mole's back feet are also webbed. The mole uses its front feet to move through the soil. Its narrow snout is pinkish white, with nostrils on the top. Fur hides the mole's eyes, which are covered in a thin layer of skin. The mole can see only changes in light. However, its other senses, including hearing, touch, and smell, are excellent. Moles live alone and build tunnel systems underground for taking shelter, raising young, and hunting.

## HOW TO SPOT

**Size:** 6.3 to 8.3 inches (16 to 21.1 cm) long including tail; 2.3 to 4.9 ounces (65 to 139 g)

**North American Range:** Southeastern South Dakota to northern Mexico

**Habitat:** Woodlands, pastures, meadows, gardens, lawns, farm fields, and areas with sandy or loamy soil

**Diet:** Insects, larvae, grubs, earthworms, and some plants

### FUN FACT

**When moles dig underground tunnels, the dirt they remove is piled in molehills near tunnel entrances.**

# NORTHERN SHORT-TAILED SHREW

*(BLARINA BREVICAUDA)*

The northern short-tailed shrew is North America's largest shrew. It has small eyes, a pointed nose, and a dark gray coat. It spends most of its time underground or buried under leaves. The northern short-tailed shrew has a neurotoxin in its saliva. This venom affects the nervous system and can be deadly to small animals such as frogs and rodents. The shrew's venom is not dangerous to humans.

## HOW TO SPOT

**Size:** 3.7 to 5.3 inches (9.4 to 13.5 cm) long including tail; 0.5 to 1 ounce (14 to 28 g)

**North American Range:** Southern Canada and eastern United States

**Habitat:** Forests, fields, and backyards

**Diet:** Grubs, insects, earthworms, snails, beetles, slugs, plants, and small mammals

# STAR-NOSED MOLE

## *(CONDYLURA CRISTATA)*

The star-nosed mole is easily recognized by its nose, which has 22 fleshy tentacles. The nearly blind mole uses its nose to find its way underground by quickly moving the tentacles against the soil. The nose holds more than 100,000 nerve fibers that sense the surroundings. The mole constantly moves and touches to find food and navigate underground tunnels. Whiskers on its head and front feet also help the mole feel its way in the darkness. Powerful shoulders and large claws help the mole dig tunnels. It makes shallow tunnels for traveling and foraging. Deeper tunnels are used to nest and shelter from cold weather.

### FUN FACT

**The star-nosed mole is the world's fastest-eating mammal. It can eat prey in less than one-fifth of a second.**

### HOW TO SPOT

**Size:** 5.9 to 8.3 inches (15 to 21.1 cm) long excluding tail; 1 to 2.6 ounces (28 to 74 g)

**North American Range:** Eastern Canada and United States

**Habitat:** Wetlands near streams, lakes, and swamps

**Diet:** Worms, grubs, insects, beetles, mollusks, amphibians, and small fish

# NINE-BANDED ARMADILLO

## *(DASYPUS NOVEMCINCTUS)*

The nine-banded armadillo gets its name from the armor-like bony plates on its body. In Spanish, *armadillo* means "little armored one." This species of armadillo has 7 to 11 bands on its armor. The armor protects the armadillo from bears, mountain lions, and other predators. The armadillo is nocturnal, spending the night burrowing and finding food. Armadillos are not picky eaters. They use their excellent sense of smell to detect nearly 500 different foods, including many types of invertebrates. The armadillo can hold its breath underwater for up to six minutes as it walks across the bottom of small streams or rivers.

### HOW TO SPOT

**Size:** 2 to 2.5 feet (0.6 to 0.8 m) long excluding tail; 8 to 17 pounds (3.6 to 7.7 kg)

**North American Range:** Southeastern United States to Panama

**Habitat:** Warm, wet climates in forests or grasslands

**Diet:** Invertebrates, small reptiles, amphibians, eggs, fruits, seeds, and other plant matter

# VIRGINIA OPOSSUM

## *(DIDELPHIS VIRGINIANA)*

The Virginia opossum is the only North American marsupial found north of Mexico. Its fur is usually white and tipped in black. The opossum is an excellent climber. It has sharp claws to dig into bark and a long tail that can grip branches. When threatened or scared, an opossum often pretends to be dead to trick predators. Virginia opossums are most active between dusk and dawn and nest in tree holes or dens abandoned by other animals. After birth, opossum babies crawl into their mother's pouch, where they continue developing. The baby opossums climb in and out of the pouch as they grow. Sometimes they ride on their mother's back as she hunts.

### HOW TO SPOT

**Size:** 2.3 to 3.3 feet (0.7 to 1 m) long including tail; 4.4 to 6.6 pounds (2 to 3 kg)

**North American Range:** Canada to Costa Rica

**Habitat:** Woodlands, thickets, wet meadows, and other habitats near a water source

**Diet:** Small mammals, birds, insects, worms, fruits, seeds, and other plant matter

# BELUGA *(DELPHINAPTERUS LEUCAS)*

Belugas are social whales that live in groups called pods, which range in size from a few whales to hundreds. The beluga has a bulbous forehead called a melon. The whale can change its facial expressions by changing the melon's shape. Belugas communicate using chirps, clicks, whistles, and squeals. Members of a pod hunt and migrate together. As sea ice forms in the fall, the pod moves south from the Arctic. It returns in the spring when the ice breaks up. Thick skin and a layer of fat called blubber insulate the beluga from the frigid waters.

## FUN FACT

**Because of the sounds it makes, the beluga is known as the "canary of the sea."**

## HOW TO SPOT

**Size:** 8.5 to 16 feet (2.6 to 4.9 m) long; 1,500 to 3,500 pounds (680 to 1,590 kg)

**North American Range:** Arctic and subarctic waters around Alaska and Canada

**Habitat:** Cold oceans, coastal bays, and inlets

**Diet:** Shrimp, crabs, mollusks, and fish such as salmon and herring

# BLUE WHALE

## *(BALAENOPTERA MUSCULUS)*

The blue whale is the largest animal on Earth. It has a long, slender body that is a mottled bluish-gray color. Blue whales typically swim alone or in pairs but occasionally travel in small groups. They generally stay in polar waters during the summer and migrate toward the warm equator in winter. Blue whales feed primarily on krill, a tiny ocean crustacean. To eat, the blue whale swims toward large schools of krill and opens its mouth. The whale then closes its mouth. Baleen plates attached to the roof of its mouth act as a filter, trapping the krill as the whale pushes the water out of its mouth.

### HOW TO SPOT

**Size:** 80 to 100 feet (24 to 30 m) long; nearly 200 short tons (180 metric tons)

**North American Range:** North Atlantic and North Pacific Oceans

**Habitat:** Oceans

**Diet:** Mainly krill, but occasionally fish and tiny crustaceans

# CALIFORNIA SEA LION

## *(ZALOPHUS CALIFORNIANUS)*

California sea lions live along the western coast of North America. Males are brown. Females and juveniles are blond or tan. Males have a forehead crest with tufts of light-colored hair. California sea lions have large front flippers that help them move through the water, and they have hind flippers with claws. The flippers help a sea lion regulate its body temperature by absorbing heat from the sun. To cool down, the sea lion dips its flipper into the water and raises it into the air. The seawater evaporates, cooling the sea lion. California sea lions are smart. They travel in groups and often relax together on beaches, piers, and jetties.

### HOW TO SPOT

**Size:** 6 to 7.5 feet (1.8 to 2.3 m) long; 240 to 700 pounds (109 to 318 kg)

**North American Range:** North Pacific Ocean coastlines

**Habitat:** Temperate or subtropical ocean waters

**Diet:** Mackerel, squid, anchovies, rockfish, salmon, and other ocean prey

### FUN FACT

To communicate, sea lions make a loud noise that sounds like a dog's bark or a lion's roar.

# COMMON BOTTLENOSE DOLPHIN

## *(TURSIOPS TRUNCATUS)*

The common bottlenose dolphin is named for its short snout. These gray dolphins can be found in temperate and tropical oceans worldwide. Bottlenose dolphins typically travel in pods and communicate with whistles and squeaks. These dolphins must surface to breathe about two to three times per minute. Bottlenose dolphins use echolocation to track prey. Female dolphins are pregnant for about a year. After giving birth, a female nurses her calf for about 20 months. A young calf remains with its mother for three to six years.

### HOW TO SPOT

**Size:** 6 to 13 feet (1.8 to 4 m) long; 300 to 1,400 pounds (136 to 635 kg)

**North American Range:** Atlantic and Pacific Oceans

**Habitat:** Ocean waters, harbors, bays, gulfs, estuaries, and coastal waters near shore

**Diet:** Fish, shrimp, and squid

# COMMON DOLPHIN

## *(DELPHINUS DELPHIS)*

The common dolphin can be found in waters worldwide. It has a rounded forehead and small flippers. Its sleek body has a triangular dorsal fin on its back. It has a long, pointed beak and jaws with many small, sharp teeth used to grab slippery fish. The dolphin's back is dark brown or black, while its underside is white or cream. A tan and light gray hourglass pattern stretches across the dolphin's side, separating the animal's back and belly colors. Common dolphins are very social and usually travel in groups of hundreds. They are often seen at the water's surface, leaping and performing flips and somersaults. They also swim next to ships.

### HOW TO SPOT

**Size:** 5 to 8 feet (1.5 to 2.4 m) long; 220 to 300 pounds (100 to 136 kg)

**North American Range:** Atlantic and Pacific Oceans

**Habitat:** Warm tropical to cool temperate coastal waters

**Diet:** Small fish, squid, and octopuses

### FUN FACT

**Dolphins show signs of sadness and grief when members of their group are separated or die.**

# HARBOR PORPOISE

## *(PHOCOENA PHOCOENA)*

The harbor porpoise is a marine mammal with a blunt nose and a triangular fin on its back. To breathe, the porpoise rises to the water's surface. It breathes through two blowholes near the top of its head. Unlike other porpoises, the shy harbor porpoise does not swim alongside boats. Typically, it does not splash when surfacing but rolls and arches its back. Harbor porpoises usually travel in pairs or small groups of up to ten animals. At times they join a larger group of up to 100 porpoises.

### HOW TO SPOT

**Size:** 5 to 5.5 feet (1.5 to 1.7 m) long; 135 to 170 pounds (61 to 77 kg)

**North American Range:** Near the North American East and West Coasts

**Habitat:** Coastal and offshore waters such as bays, estuaries, and harbors

**Diet:** Schooling fish such as herring and mackerel; occasionally squid and octopuses

# HARBOR SEAL *(PHOCA VITULINA)*

Harbor seals are commonly spotted along US coasts, resting on rocks, beaches, and glacial ice. They have short flippers, a short snout, and small ear openings on each side of their head. Some harbor seals are light tan or silver with dark spots or markings. Others have darker-colored fur with light markings. A thick layer of fat called blubber keeps them warm in cold waters. In the water, harbor seals are graceful swimmers. They can sleep underwater, surfacing for air only every 30 minutes. On land, harbor seals are not as graceful. Because they cannot use their hind flippers to walk, the seals move in a wave like a caterpillar.

## HOW TO SPOT

**Size:** 5 to 6 feet (1.5 to 1.8 m) long; 180 to 285 pounds (82 to 129 kg)

**North American Range:** Northern coasts of North America

**Habitat:** Coastal habitats

**Diet:** Fish, shellfish, and crustaceans

# HOODED SEAL *(CYSTOPHORA CRISTATA)*

Hooded seals are large. They are named for the adult male's stretchy hood in his nose. The male can inflate this hood, which looks like a red balloon. The male seal uses the hood to attract females and to warn off other males. Hooded seals are solitary except during breeding season and molting season, which is when they lose their fur and new fur grows. They have silver-gray fur and irregular dark spots. These seals can dive deep and stay underwater for up to one hour.

**FUN FACT**

**Hooded seal mothers nurse their pups for only three to five days after birth, which is the shortest nursing period for a mammal.**

Female

Hood

## HOW TO SPOT

**Size:** 6.5 to 8.5 feet (2 to 2.6 m) long; 320 to 776 pounds (145 to 352 kg)

**North American Range:** North Atlantic and Arctic Oceans

**Habitat:** Coastal areas of Atlantic and Arctic Oceans

**Diet:** Fish, octopuses, and shrimp

# HUMPBACK WHALE

## *(MEGAPTERA NOVAEANGLIAE)*

The humpback whale is named for the hump on its back. This large, black whale with white markings is popular with whale watchers because it often jumps out of the water and slaps the surface with its fins or tail. During spring and summer, humpback whales spend most of their time finding food. They must build up the fat stores that support them through the winter, when there is less food. Humpback whales travel far during their annual migration between summer feeding grounds and winter breeding areas. Some whales swim 5,000 miles (8,047 km) between the two. They are social animals and are often seen in groups.

### HOW TO SPOT

**Size:** 60 feet (18 m) long; 40 short tons (36 metric tons)
**North American Range:** Atlantic and Pacific Oceans
**Habitat:** Coastal and open ocean waters
**Diet:** Small fish and crustaceans such as krill

### WHALE SONGS

Humpback whales are known for their mysterious underwater songs. To sing, the whales make a series of complex sounds such as moans, howls, cries, and other noises. Their songs differ from regular calls associated with feeding or social behaviors. The songs are longer and have a defined structure with repetitive parts sung in a specific sequence. Scientists are studying the whales' songs to understand their meaning.

# NARWHAL *(MONODON MONOCEROS)*

The narwhal is an Arctic marine mammal known for the long spiral tusk protruding from its head, which is actually an elongated tooth. Males grow tusks that can reach ten feet (3 m) long. Narwhals live in the Arctic's icy waters. They have a mottled gray body and no dorsal fin, so they can easily navigate under sea ice. Narwhals breathe through cracks in sea ice when needed. They can dive up to 1.5 miles (2.4 km) deep. They live in pods and communicate with clicks and whistles.

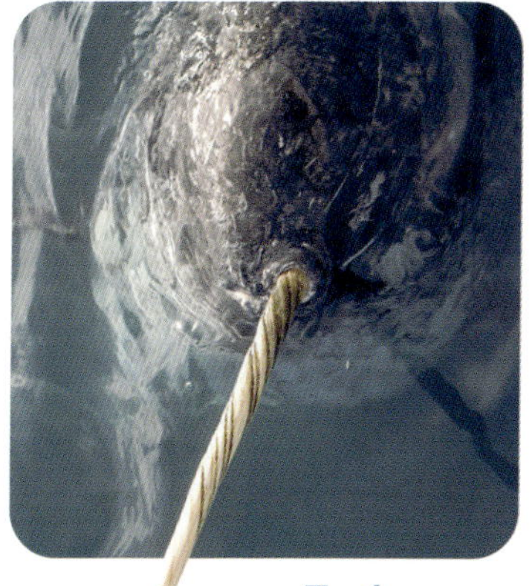

Tusk

## HOW TO SPOT

**Size:** 13 to 18 feet (4 to 5.5 m) long; 1,760 to 3,530 pounds (800 to 1,600 kg)

**North American Range:** Arctic Ocean from central Canada to Greenland

**Habitat:** Cold Arctic Ocean

**Diet:** Halibut, Arctic and polar cod, squid, and shrimp

# NORTHERN FUR SEAL

## *(CALLORHINUS URSINUS)*

The northern fur seal has a stocky body and a small head. Its fur is very thick, and whiskers extend from its snout. Its front flippers are powerful, and the seal uses them to walk, run, and swim. The seals range in color from dark brown to black in males and dark gray to brown in females. Northern fur seals live in the open ocean. They spend more than 300 days each year at sea. They come to land to rest, mate, and raise their young. This seal is primarily solitary and can be aggressive on land, especially during mating season.

### HOW TO SPOT

**Size:** 5 to 7 feet (1.5 to 2.1 m) long; 120 to 600 pounds (54 to 272 kg)

**North American Range:** Oceans near North America's West Coast

**Habitat:** Open ocean and rocky or sandy beaches

**Diet:** Fish and squid

# ORCA *(ORCINUS ORCA)*

The orca, also known as the killer whale, is a powerful and intelligent marine predator found in oceans worldwide. Orcas are the largest members of the dolphin family. Their black-and-white coloring makes them easily recognizable. Orcas are highly social. They live in pods, which include up to 40 members. Orcas make various sounds to communicate, and each pod uses unique sounds so group members can find each other. They use echolocation and teamwork to hunt.

## HOW TO SPOT

**Size:** 23 to 32 feet (7 to 9.8 m) long; up to 11 short tons (10 metric tons)

**North American Range:** Atlantic and Pacific Oceans

**Habitat:** Coastal and open ocean waters

**Diet:** Fish, birds, squid, octopuses, and marine mammals such as seals, dolphins, and whales

## FUN FACT

Ancient sailors watched groups of orcas hunting large whale species and gave them the name killer whale.

# RINGED SEAL *(PUSA HISPIDA)*

The ringed seal is a small, common Arctic seal. It gets its name from the distinctive light rings on its darker coat. Ringed seals spend much of their time close to shore ice. They use claws on their front flippers to dig cone-shaped breathing holes in the ice. The seals can dive deep into the ocean and stay underwater for up to 45 minutes. Ringed seals are solitary mammals and gather on sea ice only to mate and rest. When there is enough snow, these seals build snow caves. A female gives birth in a snow cave, which protects the new pup from predators and extreme cold.

## HOW TO SPOT

**Size:** 4 to 4.5 feet (1.2 to 1.4 m) long; 110 to 150 pounds (50 to 68 kg)

**North American Range:** Arctic Ocean and neighboring seas

**Habitat:** Polar oceans

**Diet:** Small fish and crustaceans

## FUN FACT

**Before they surface, ringed seals sometimes blow bubbles through their breathing holes. If a polar bear is waiting on the ice above, it might react to the bubbles, and the seal can escape.**

# SHORT-FINNED PILOT WHALE

## *(GLOBICEPHALA MACRORHYNCHUS)*

Short-finned pilot whales are large, social dolphins. They have a distinctive bulbous forehead and dark-brown or black coloring. Pilot whales live in family pods of 15 to 30 animals and are known for their strong social bonds. They spend their days resting and traveling. The whales feed at night, traveling a large area looking for food. Pilot whales are nicknamed the "cheetahs of the deep sea" because they dive at high speed when hunting large squid.

### HOW TO SPOT

**Size:** 12 to 24 feet (3.7 to 7.3 m) long; 1.1 to 3.3 short tons (1 to 3 metric tons)

**North American Range:** Atlantic and Pacific Oceans

**Habitat:** Deep ocean and coastal waters

**Diet:** Squid and small fish

# WALRUS *(ODOBENUS ROSMARUS)*

The walrus is a large marine mammal with whiskers, long tusks, and a blubbery body. The social walrus is typically found in Arctic regions lying on the ice with hundreds of other walruses. The group members often bellow loudly and snort at each other. Walruses use their tusks to help pull their massive bodies from the water onto ice or land. They also use their tusks to make breathing holes in the ice. Males use their tusks to defend territory or protect females during mating season. The walrus's blubber insulates it in the cold Arctic region.

## HOW TO SPOT

**Size:** 7.3 to 11.5 feet (2.2 to 3.5 m) long; 1,320 to 3,310 pounds (600 to 1,500 kg)
**North American Range:** Arctic regions
**Habitat:** Arctic ice and shallow Arctic waters
**Diet:** Small invertebrates such as mollusks

# WEST INDIAN MANATEE

## *(TRICHECHUS MANATUS)*

The West Indian manatee, often called a sea cow, is a large, gentle marine mammal that lives in shallow coastal waters and rivers. The manatee has paddle-shaped flippers, a rounded tail, and wrinkled skin. Manatees move slowly and spend much of their time eating, resting, and migrating. Despite their size, manatees are graceful swimmers with strong tails that propel them through the water. They live alone or in pairs or small groups. Manatees live entirely in the water but must breathe air at the water's surface. When resting, a manatee can stay underwater for up to 15 minutes. When swimming, it must surface to breathe every three to four minutes.

### HOW TO SPOT

**Size:** 8 to 13 feet (2.4 to 4 m) long; 440 to 3,310 pounds (200 to 1,500 kg)

**North American Range:** East Coast from Florida to Panama

**Habitat:** Rivers, bays, canals, estuaries, and coastal areas in both fresh and salt water

**Diet:** Water grasses, weeds, and algae

# GLOSSARY

**aggressive**
Marked by self-assertiveness or a readiness to attack.

**alpine**
Relating to high elevations where trees cannot grow.

**camouflage**
The ability to blend in with the surroundings.

**domestic**
Bred to be tame and useful to people.

**flank**
The side of an animal between the ribs and hip.

**forage**
To search for food.

**gland**
An organ or group of cells that releases substances for the body to use or get rid of.

**grizzled**
Streaked with gray hair.

**hibernate**
To spend the winter in a resting state.

**insulate**
To protect from the transfer of heat.

**juvenile**
A young or immature individual.

**membrane**
A thin, flexible layer of skin or other tissue.

**pathogen**
An agent such as a virus or bacterium that causes disease.

**solitary**
Preferring to be alone.

**subspecies**
A group within a species that lives in a certain geographic region and is genetically distinct from other members of that species.

**taiga**
A subarctic forest of mostly conifers.

**territorial**
Describing an animal that defends its home range from others.

**tundra**
A cold, treeless region found mostly north of the Arctic Circle.

**typically**
Usually.

# TO LEARN MORE

## FURTHER READINGS


Clutton-Brock, Juliet. *Cat*. DK, 2022.

Drimmer, Stephanie Warren. *Ultimate Mammalpedia*. National Geographic Kids, 2023.

Spelman, Lucy. *Animal Encyclopedia*. National Geographic, 2021.


## ONLINE RESOURCES

To learn more about North American mammals, please visit **abdobooklinks.com** or scan this QR code. These links are routinely monitored and updated to provide the most current information available.

# PHOTO CREDITS

Cover Photos: Shutterstock Images, front (bear, seal, dolphin, skunk, chipmunk, weasel, moose, ocelot, fox, wolf), back (armadillo, squirrel); McDonald Wildlife Photography Inc./The Image Bank/Getty Images, front (bat)
Interior Photos: Shutterstock Images, 1 (goat), 5 (jaguar), 5 (dolphins), 5 (opossum), 6, 7, 10, 11 (bottom), 12, 13 (bottom), 14, 15 (bottom), 16 (right), 31, 33, 34, 36, 40, 48 (bottom), 52, 63, 65 (left), 65 (right), 73, 76, 77, 79 (bottom), 90 (bottom), 92, 95, 98 (top), 98 (bottom), 99 (top), 103 (bottom), 112 (skunk); Eric Isselee/Shutterstock Images, 1 (musk ox), 1 (cat), 4 (rat), 4 (porcupine), 5 (raccoon), 18, 28, 32 (right), 37, 38, 68, 80, 112 (fox); Michal Pesata/Shutterstock Images, 1 (ermine), 46 (top); Jody Ann/Shutterstock Images, 1 (beaver), 66; Holly Kuchera/Shutterstock Images, 4 (mink), 44, 47; Natalia Volkova/Shutterstock Images, 5 (bear), 53; Randy Bjorklund/Shutterstock Images, 5 (rabbit), 64, 91; Darren Baker/Shutterstock Images, 8; Tory Kallman/Shutterstock Images, 9 (top), 103 (top); Bonnie Fink/Shutterstock Images, 9 (bottom); Jeffrey T. Kreulen/Shutterstock Images, 11 (top); Robert Harding Video/Shutterstock Images, 13 (top); Petr Simon/Shutterstock Images, 15 (top); Andre Anita/Shutterstock Images, 16 (left); Stephen J. Krasemann/Science Source, 17 (left); Ivan Kuzmin/Science Source, 17 (right); Dennis W. Donohue/Shutterstock Images, 19, 54; Paul Tessier/Shutterstock Images, 20; Danita Delimont/Shutterstock Images, 21 (left); Michael Tatman/Shutterstock Images, 21 (right); Alexey Seafarer/Shutterstock Images, 22 (top); Ondrej Prosicky/Shutterstock Images, 22 (bottom), 51; Warren Metcalf/Shutterstock Images, 23, 42; Michael Weber/imageBROKER/Blue Planet Archive, 24; Travis Potter/Shutterstock Images, 25, 43, 71 (top), 84 (bottom); Dennis Fast/VW Pics/Universal Images Group/Getty Images, 26; Rick & Nora Bowers/Alamy, 27; Mark Newman/Lonely Planet RF/Getty Images, 29; Geoffrey Kuchera/Shutterstock Images, 30; Kathleen Reeder Wildlife Photography/Moment/Getty Images, 32 (left); Juan Carlos Vindas/Moment/Getty Images, 35; McDonald Wildlife Photography Inc./The Image Bank/Getty Images, 39, 58, 112 (bat); David Havel/Shutterstock Images, 41; Kerry Hargrove/

Shutterstock Images, 45 (top); Kerry Hargrove/iStockphoto, 45 (bottom); Stephan Morris/ Shutterstock Images, 46 (bottom); Griffin Gillespie/ Shutterstock Images, 48 (top); Jukka Jantunen/Shutterstock Images, 49; Henner Damke/ Shutterstock Images, 50 (top); Richard Fitzer/Shutterstock Images, 50 (bottom); Himanshu Saraf/Shutterstock Images, 55; Jay Ondreicka/Shutterstock Images, 56; MerlinTuttle.org/ Science Source, 57 (left), 57 (right), 59; Arterra/Universal Images Group/Getty Images, 60; Sophia Granchinho/Shutterstock Images, 61 (top); Dan Bach Kristensen/Shutterstock Images, 61 (bottom); Melinda Fawver/ Shutterstock Images, 62; Mircea Costina/Shutterstock Images, 67, 79 (top); Nick Pecker/Shutterstock Images, 69, 102; Phil A. Dotson/Science Source, 70; Elliotte Rusty Harold/Shutterstock Images, 71 (bottom); iStockphoto, 72; Leena Robinson/Shutterstock Images, 74 (top), 74 (bottom); Colin Varndell/Science Source, 75; Agnieszka Bacal/Shutterstock Images, 78 (top); Gary Meszaros/ Science Source, 78 (bottom); Tom McHugh/Science Source, 81 (top); Richard R. Hansen/Science Source, 81 (bottom); Georgi Baird/Shutterstock Images, 82; Kenneth W. Fink/Science Source, 83; Stan Tekiela Author/ Naturalist/Wildlife Photographer/ Moment/Getty Images, 84 (top); John Serrao/Science Source, 85; E. R. Degginger/ Science Source, 86; Liz Weber/ Shutterstock Images, 87; Scott Camazine/Science Source, 88; Skip Moody/Science Source, 89; Marcelo Morena/Shutterstock Images, 90 (top); Andrew Sutton/ Shutterstock Images, 93; Jesus Cobaleda/Shutterstock Images, 94 (top); Martin Prochazkacz/ Shutterstock Images, 94 (bottom); Michael Patrick O'Neill/ Science Source, 96; Nick Hawkins/NaturePL/Science Source, 97; M. Watson/Science Source, 99 (bottom); David Fleetham/Stocktrek Images/ Science Source, 100 (left); Gudkov Andrey/Shutterstock Images, 100 (right); Bryan & Cherry Alexander/Blue Planet Archive, 101 (top); Doc White/ Blue Planet Archive, 101 (bottom); Sergey Uryadnikov/Shutterstock Images, 104; Sergio Hanquet/ Science Source, 105; Christopher Wood/Shutterstock Images, 106; Thierry Eidenweil/Shutterstock Images, 107

**ABDOBOOKS.COM**
Published by Abdo Reference, a division of ABDO, PO Box 398166, Minneapolis, Minnesota 55439. 

Printed in China.
052025
092025

Editor: Marie Pearson
Series Designer: Colleen McLaren
Production Designer: Laura Kuchar

**LIBRARY OF CONGRESS CONTROL NUMBER: 2024949010**
**PUBLISHER'S CATALOGING-IN-PUBLICATION DATA**
Names: Mooney, Carla, author.
Title: Mammals / by Carla Mooney
Description: Minneapolis, Minnesota: Abdo Reference, 2026 | Series: North American field guides | Includes online resources and index.
Identifiers: ISBN 9781098297688 (lib. bdg.) | ISBN 9798384930204 (ebook)
Subjects: LCSH: Mammals--Juvenile literature. | Mammals--Behavior--Juvenile literature. | Animal--Juvenile literature. | Zoology--Juvenile literature. | Reference materials--Juvenile literature.
Classification: DDC 599--dc23